The Official Alien Abductee's Handbook

The Official Alien Abductee's Handbook

How to Recover from Alien Abductions without Hypnotherapy, Crystals, or CIA Surveillance

Joe Tripician

illustrations by
Lawrence Christmas

Andrews and McMeel

A Universal Press Syndicate Company
Kansas City

Designed by Randall Blair Design.

Library of Congress Cataloging-in-Publication Data
Tripician, Joseph.
    The official alien abductee's handbook: how to recover from alien abductions without hypnotherapy, crystals, or CIA surveillance / by Joe Tripician; illustrations by Lawrence Christmas.
        p. cm.
    ISBN 0-8362-2760-3 (pbk.)
    1. Alien abduction—Humor. I. Title
BF2050.T75 1997
001.942'02'07—dc21

For Mom and Dad

ACKNOWLEDGMENTS

Many thanks to my agent, Superwoman Rosalind Lichter, who can leap tall contracts in a single bound. Bountiful thanks to my editor Jake Morrissey, who I had more fun telling alien stories to than any night around the Boy Scout campfire. Much thanks also to Regan Brown, Cynthia Borg, Chris Pizey, Nora Donaghy, and all the other true believers at A&M.

For their contributions and suggestions I gratefully thank former coconspirator Merrill Aldighieri, fellow satirist Curtis Ellis, ectoplasmic archer Edward C. Cornell, and melody man Frederick Reed.

Thanks to Muppet alumnus Sal Denaro for turning me onto the amazing Lawrence Christmas, illustrator extraordinaire. Thanks also to Lisa Fonfrias for her terrific inking. To design mavens Andrea Hopp and Joe Trainor. To Liz Ziemska and Nick Ellison for being the first to "get it," and to Mark Rubin for publishing advice.

To my friends: Kathy Brew, Nancy Cohen, Barbara Crane, Simon and Celeste Grome, Jacky and Intensity Kamhaji, Hillary Lane, Ellen Colón Lugo, Harriet Martin, Tom Murrin, "The Alien Comic" and Patricia Sullivan, Grai St. Claire Rice, Amy Rosemarin, Hannah Silverman, Kathy Singer, Rob Steiner, Edin Velez, and Sarah Venable.

Eternal gratitude to Bill Tripician for first infecting me with the showbiz bug, and to Carl Tripician for his lawyerly advice and brotherly counsel.

Thanks to my parents, Delores and Nick, for countless reasons.

CONTENTS

Foreword ....**xv**

Introduction ....**xvii**

What to Expect Before You Take Your Trip 1

Getting Ready for Your Trip 4

Have You Been Abducted? Quiz #1..5

The Ten Telltale Signs That You Have Been Abducted...........................6

How to Diss an Alien 7

The Top Ten Reasons You Have Been Chosen to Be Abducted 8

What to Tell Your Doctor (Without Getting Yourself Committed) 9

How to Interpret Alien Gestures...10

How to Translate Alien Symbols 12

Motives 13

Monitoring Your Feelings 14

Scoop Dreams..16

How to Speak with Plainclothes Government Personnel 17

Inside the Black Box..18

The Incubatorium 20

How to Deal with the Public...22

The Seven Basic Types of ETs...23

The Alien Abductor's Checklist...27

How to Appear on Talk Shows 30

Why Nonabductees Don't Believe 32

Alien Sex 34

How to Tell Your Fiancée 36

Abductee Sex...37

How to Pick Up Abductee Chicks................................39

How to Break Up with Your Abductee Boyfriend 41

Abductee Personals...43

How to Avoid Being Abducted 46

Near-Death Experiences and Alien Abductions 48

The Lighter Side of Alien Abductions 49

Alien Abduction of Children 50

Alien Abductee Nursery Rhymes.................................51

Staging 53

Media Display..55

Mindscan...58

Screen Memory 59

Hypnotic Regression 60

Postabduction Syndrome 62

False-Memory Syndrome...63

Have You Been Abducted? Quiz #2.............................65

Conspiracies À Go-Go..66

Psy-Ops and PC Bashing 68

Mind Control, American Style 70

A Male Alien Abductee's Diary 73

A Female Alien Abductee's Diary 76

"Abductee in the U.S.A." 78

Cow Mutilations 80

Foo Fighters 82

The Men in Black..84

The Space Brothers 86

Joe Simonton's Intergalactic House of Pancakes 88

Divine Invasions 90

Preparing for the Inevitable 93

The Psychological Profile of an ET Abductor 95

How to Abduct Your Very Own Alien...97

Alien Infiltrators in Our Culture 98

The New-Age Comic..100

The Stockholm Syndrome 102

Genitalia Envy 104

Angel vs. Aliens...105

Chariots of the Creeps 108

The Official Alien Abductee Hotline 110

Last Exit to Roswell 111

An Alien at My (Autopsy) Table 114

Ten Uses for a Dead Alien 116

A Dreamland of Dollars..117

Alien Abductee Glossary 119

About the Author 123

FOREWORD

by Xenob the High Pleiadian

(as channeled through Joe Tripician)

Very clever. Very clever, indeed. This document you hold in
your hands is either an elaborate hoax perpetrated by a publicity-
starved miscreant, or a leaked classified government file designed
to slowly indoctrinate the public into a widespread acceptance of
our visiting race. Oh, so very clever. It must, of course, be
destroyed.

INTRODUCTION

Aliens visiting Earth? Seeking humans of all ages, races, and sizes? Abducting them and submitting them to various intrusive "medical" tests—and not even billing them? Whether you believe in UFOs, aliens, Whitley Strieber, or universal health care, most of us are unprepared to be abducted by aliens (hell, most of us are unprepared for children, middle age, and tax audits). So, this book is meant as a handguide should you be abducted—which will make your next tax audit a cakewalk by comparison.

The author has spent many protracted minutes exhaustively researching the field of alien abductions to come up with this handy guide, a road map, if you will, to your:
• Journey of Abduction by Superpowerful Alien Creatures
• Restraint under Unknown Medical Procedures
• Loss of Memory
• Eventual Subjugation to Ridicule by Nonabductees.

The typical abductee* will spend years in dysfunctional relationships, dead-end jobs, and simple physiological pain before realizing something's amiss. It is only after prolonged and expensive hypnosis therapy that the abductee will recover the torturous and horrific memory of their abduction. Soon, bodily scars and inexplicable phobias suddenly have a cause—albeit a cause more often associated with dementia and featherbrains, but a cause nonetheless.

* *The author prefers the term "abductee," as opposed to the more trendy, New-Agey "experiencer." And while "experiencer" may put the mind at ease if you happen to be the one experiencing forced alien encounters, I just wonder whose experience you'd really rather have?*

The author, by way of disclosure, has never been abducted—he's never even seen a UFO (unless you count that night in Guadalajara with the midget and the chicken foot). I hold to no particular theories or beliefs about UFOs except to remain skeptically gullible, our best defense against an increasingly complex future. And, if reports of UFOs, crop circles, alien abductions, unexplained cow mutilations, line dancing, and other impenetrable and inexplicable phenomena continue, you might want to remain a little open-minded; it could prove useful should you be abducted—or even asked to examine those strange scars behind your lover's ears.

Reports of alien abductions now number into the thousands—of those willing to divulge their episodes. (In this regard alien abduction may be akin to masturbation: The people who admit to it are vastly smaller in number those who actually engage in it.) Thus, the chances could be as low as one in ten that you will be abducted, already have been abducted, or a close relative or friend will be abducted (in which case you should buy them extra copies of this book).

The author hopes that, as you read this guide, as you travel through the pain, coercion, humiliation, and despair, you receive a little solace from its underlying advice—just relax and go with it—after all, you have no choice!

WHAT TO EXPECT BEFORE
YOU TAKE YOUR TRIP

Survival tips for the cosmically challenged.

1) THE APPEARANCE
Chipper exhibitionists or cosmic muggers?
A disc or oval-shaped object will appear in the sky followed by
bright flashes of blinding white light(s). If you are driving,
your car will suddenly become disabled. If you are walking,
your arms and legs will suddenly become disabled. If you are
thinking, your mind will suddenly become disabled.

2) THE CAPTURE
The hunt for Homo Sapiens as a shoplifting spree.
One or several four-foot, gray-white, hairless humanoid
beings with almond bug-eyes, large heads, long limbs, and
Kate Moss torsos will appear to escort you effortlessly (sometimes levitating you) into their spacecraft as you silently
scream in unbridled terror.

3) THE FIVE-CENT TOUR
On the whole I'd rather be just about anywhere else.
Once inside, your hosts may take the opportunity to show you
their diabolically superior space technology, which generally
adds to your feelings of powerlessness, persecution, and
estrangement (you know, "alien"-nation). This is probably
intended to intimidate those who haven't already soiled themselves.

4) THE FREE MEDICAL EXAM
Close encounters of the third degree.
You will be strapped onto a large, downy-white table and will undergo an excruciatingly painful, hopelessly humiliating, and extensively intrusive "medical" exam. Long, thin metallic poles and needles will be stuck into every orifice. New orifices will be created. Tissue samples of your vital internal organs will be taken as souvenirs. A fun time will be had by all.

5) MISSING TIME
Picture your memory on the sides of milk cartons.
Don't worry too much about all the pain, humiliation, and abuse you've suffered, because you won't remember it! The aliens have perfected a technique that erases your memory, leaving it emptier than a Pentagon expense account before an appropriations hearing. You'll be left with gaps of "missing time" as your only memento. Hours will have passed before you notice yourself walking down a gravel road with your clothes on backward.

6) REGRESSIVE HYPNOSIS
Total recall is just a breakdown away.
You can reclaim your memory through a psycho-therapeutic process where you are hypnotized by a licensed therapist. Those deeply buried experiences will be dredged up for a complete review by someone who, with just a flick of his pen, can put you away for the rest of your life. That's why most abductees only visit self-trained therapists who specialize in abductions, and who will record every horrific and humiliating detail and publish it for the whole world to enjoy.

7) THE RETURN TRIP

"Earth is so nice, we had to visit twice," seems to be the aliens' motto. "Your ass is now mine" would probably be more appropriate, for our intrepid intruders seem awfully partial to the use of brain implants. These little devices of unknown material are implanted in your skull and act as homing beacons to bring your hosts back again and again—to sample your wares and generally treat you the way we treat our very own animals on the planet. Lobotomy, anyone?

GETTING READY FOR YOUR TRIP

Destination: Subjugation!

What to wear: It won't matter. Our alien's sense of fashion is limited to materials not found on this planet. But easy access to your rump will cut down the travel time.

What to bring: It won't matter since they won't let you bring anything, especially cameras, audio recording equipment, and of course your memory.

HAVE YOU BEEN ABDUCTED?

Quiz #1

1) WHEN YOU SLEEP YOU DREAM OF:
   a) Floating serenely about the bedroom
   b) Flying freely in the clear blue sky
   c) Being paralyzed and shoved into a round white oven

2) WHEN YOU PASS A CHILDREN'S CLOTHING STORE YOU:
   a) Smile sweetly at the tiny apparel
   b) Sigh nostalgically at remembering your childhood
   c) Break out into hives and scream, "Not again!"

3) WHEN ASKED TO GO ON A TRIP YOU:
   a) Accept with immediate alacrity
   b) Suggest a warm climate
   c) Bring along a camera crew and armed guards

THE TEN TELLTALE SIGNS THAT YOU HAVE BEEN ABDUCTED

1) You experience hefty gaps of missing time without the benefit of controlled substances.
2) A decreased sperm count or unexplained loss of eggs, even though you don't live near a nuclear power plant.
3) Sudden paranoia during laser light shows and colon exams.
4) You set off airport alarms without passing through them.
5) Plainclothes government agents seem awfully interested in you now.
6) An unexpected appetite for heavy metal—as food, not music.
7) You turn pale while watching Mighty Morphin Power Rangers.
8) You experience telepathy with common household plants.
9) After a sleepless night you awake with crop circles under your eyes.
10) Your doctor finds a map of Pluto in your anus.

HOW TO DISS AN ALIEN

- Say, "Yo, Gumby!"
- Tell them you liked them better when they were in *Deliverance*.
- Say, "At least the tribe from Betelgeuse had designer table-tops."
- Tell them you've seen better spaceships in Toys-Я-Us.
- "For a superintelligent race, you came here at the wrong millennium."
- Say, "Weren't you in The Village People?"

THE TOP TEN REASONS YOU HAVE BEEN CHOSEN TO BE ABDUCTED

Perhaps the single most-asked question by abductees is, "Why me?" (Well, actually that's the second most asked question; the single most asked question is, "What the hell are these red scars doing on my body?") Though there are many answers, here are the ones overheard most frequently on the local alien abductee hotline. (Thanks to "Big Bob" Hogan for the friendly wiretaps.)

10) Your ass is cute.
9) Your name has been specially selected by Publishers Clearinghouse.
8) Their last abductee only fed four.
7) It was so hot when they were passing through that they needed a quick dip in your gene pool.
6) That's how IRS agents are recruited.
5) There's something about you that reminds them of Michael Jackson.
4) Xenob the driver had a little too much liquid coolant last night.
3) Whitley Strieber is on a book tour.
2) Because you didn't take the hint about the cow mutilations and become a vegetarian.
1) "Because we can!"

WHAT TO TELL YOUR DOCTOR (WITHOUT GETTING YOURSELF COMMITTED)

"I heard high colonics were good for you."
"I sobered up halfway through my tattoo parlor visit."

HOW TO INTERPRET ALIEN GESTURES

"Greetings."

"Walk this way."

"Who does your nails?"

**"We are just
visiting here."**

**"Would you care
to dance?"**

**"Spread 'em,
please."**

HOW TO TRANSLATE ALIEN SYMBOLS

"Restricted Area:
Aliens Only"

"Humans Welcome"

"Please Leave Your
Memory at the Door"

MOTIVES

Alien abduction is part of their grand plan. The question is— which grand plan?

1) To prevent us from nuclear destruction, the extinction of the entire human race, and the production of any more *Barney* TV shows.
2) To cultivate an organic human food farm.
3) To control and shape our evolution to their liking and their shade of skin (come to think of it, that's also Pat Buchanan's plan).
4) To breed with us like some cheap genetic mink market and then sell our hides to fur-free designers.
5) Two millennia ago they left some bad seed here and have returned to atone by sharing with us their superior technology and guiding us toward peace, harmony, and bliss.
6) Two millennia ago they left some bad seed here and have returned to claim custody—of all of us.
7) To open a new theme park—Extinction Center.
8) It gets real lonely traveling light-years in space and they just need someone to hold, cuddle, and nibble on through the night.
9) It somehow fits into Iran-Contra, but Reagan had an episode of missing time and couldn't remember.
10) If you really knew, you'd be harder to find than a dead alien in the Pentagon.

MONITORING YOUR FEELINGS
How you should scientifically feel about your abduction.

You're confused, agitated, and not a little bit miffed. You have experienced an overwhelming event more frightening than the latest medical report from Philip Morris. To help you calmly assess the damage, simply break down your experience into two columns:

WHY YOU SHOULD FEEL GOOD ABOUT BEING ABDUCTED	WHY YOU SHOULD FEEL BAD ABOUT BEING ABDUCTED
The incredible light show.	The lingering astigmatism.
The thorough medical checkup.	The permanent physical scars.
The feelings of acceptance by an alien race, and usefulness to cosmic understanding.	The feelings of rejection and humiliation by humans at home.
You should feel privileged that you are one of the select few chosen by the aliens and brought aboard their intergalactic spacecraft . . .	. . . then dumped unceremoniously in a trailer court with your memory erased.
The coming millennium of peace, wisdom, and harmony between the species.	The coming apocalyptic War Between the Species and the Destruction of the Human Race as we know it.

You can now conduct seminars for high pay at New Age conventions.

Cheaper than Club Med, and you won't have to go to any toga parties.

You must undergo special interrogation by unnamed government agents.

Expensive hypnotherapy, unending ridicule, and the constant threat of repeat abductions hovers over you every day, no matter where you try to hide.

SCOOP DREAMS

Take another little piece of my spleen now, baby.

Our alien intruders apparently like to remove pieces from their abductees, leaving body scars called "scoop marks" on legs, arms, behind the ears, and other places best seen only by your proctologist. This fillet technique is usually accomplished with the assistance of long, thin, rodlike instruments (and the ever-popular black box). No one knows, but perhaps they are borrowing our skin and tissue as medical samples to improve the genetics on this planet or to repopulate their own anemic gene pool. Or maybe these intrepid galaxy-hoppers just want a souvenir—to remind them of the good times. In any case, be content to know that part of your pituitary gland is either being used for the prolongation of a species, or is now adorning some space tourist's dashboard.

HOW TO SPEAK WITH PLAINCLOTHES GOVERNMENT PERSONNEL

The truth vs. national security.

If any of the UFO conspiracy theories are to be believed, the government is covering up its (complicit) knowledge of our petite gray-skinned visitors. It is therefore best to divulge nothing of your close encounters (unless you are destitute and homeless and feel like a diet of Thorazine in an environment of white cinder blocks).

INSIDE THE BLACK BOX
(A skeptical disclosure.)

Stories abound of aliens randomly planting black box symbols as signs of their ▮▮▮▮▮ presence. Although the ▮▮▮▮▮ author has, ▮▮▮▮ up to now, scrupulously ▮▮▮▮▮▮ maintained his ▮▮▮▮▮ ▮▮▮ impartiality, he must take a stand and decry this absurdity. ▮▮▮▮▮▮ ▮▮▮ ▮▮▮▮▮

Possible uses for the Alien's Little Black Box:

1) Mind control, including posthypnotic suggestions such as: "Be kind to all animals, work for world peace, and fatten those thighs, will you?"

2) Transportation: The mysterious black box could contain a highly advanced conveyance technology capable of hauling large pieces of freshly killed meat over long distances.

3) Vacation snapshots: For remembering those carefree days on the human dude ranch.

4) Weapon: The possible varieties of lethal and nonlethal uses could include radiation sickness, temporary or permanent amnesia, muscle and nerve immobilizer, and microbe-induced chronic dandruff.

5) Universal medical salve: Good for what ails you. Order now and receive a free alien abductee homing pager in your choice of colors: Ganymede Gray, Fright White, and Supine Sienna.

THE INCUBATORIUM
Nothing says lovin' like something from the genetically altered oven.

The aliens' plan for breeding leads inevitably to their hothouse of human-ET cross-pollination—the Incubatorium. This factory for producing hybrid babies is so efficient it makes a Japanese car factory look like the U.S. Post Office. Nestled securely in the heart of the alien mother ship, the Incubatorium is part high-tech hospital, part satanic fish farm.

There is an operating table where the female abductee undergoes fetal extraction by two or three attending aliens. To make the mother more comfortable, a female handmaid (also an abductee) is usually present. (Her attempts at calming the mother's nerves by hand holding and cooing are not quite as effective as the massive quantities of alien drugs pumped into the patient.)

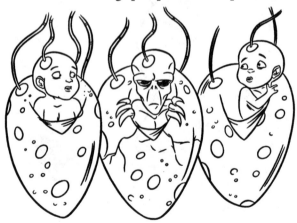

The aliens remove the fetus by placing between your legs a mechanical device that looks like a silver waterpick, but feels like a cast-iron vacuum cleaner. Should you find yourself laboring under this procedure, it might be best to simply imagine a tooth extraction, or the removal of a benign cancer—anything other than the tractor-pull happening below your navel.

When the fetus is taken out it is immediately immersed inside a large glass test tube surrounded by as many as two hundred other glass test tubes. Inside each of the cylinders are other fetuses suspended in a jellylike liquid like so many bald gerbils. Wires and tubing of various colors extend from these incubating hatcheries as an otherworldly bubbling sound echoes throughout the mother ship's hull. All in all an extremely pleasant nativity scene. In this nefarious nursery the baby incubates, growing bigger until it's a healthy, happy, hairless humanoid with its mother's soft mouth, and its father's chitinous eyes.

This assembly-line method of population growth increases the number of hybrid babies. Like the rest of alien folklore, theories abound as to how these terrestrial-seeking toddlers will be put to use once they get as big as a towering five feet. Choose your favorite from among the following possible uses of hybrids:
a) Scab airline workers on all international and domestic flights
b) Dental assistants
c) Scientology recruiters
d) CFOs of tax-exempt charitable organizations
e) To fill the endless lines of foot soldiers and cheerleaders during the alien victory parade
f) CNN news anchors.

HOW TO DEAL WITH THE PUBLIC

Tell your uptown friends you're recalling memories of a past molestation.

Tell your downtown friends you're really getting into scarification.

While most of us have loving family and friends who are emotionally supportive and sympathetic, most of us have never admitted to being abducted by vertically-challenged intergalactic proctologists. Suffice to say that what you have experienced as a blood-curdling, mind-shattering, and life-changing event of cosmic significance, your spouse just sees as a warped attempt to conceal a late-night binge. The risks of outing yourself as an abductee are as serious as they are obvious. While your coworkers may believe your story of bright lights in the sky, they may doubt the part about you lying naked while a half-dozen white-skinned ETs poke inside you. And even though you know how you got those scars, you might just prevaricate and tell your boss your date last night was an *animal!*

For those of you who hold truth higher than social acceptance, the author has the following suggestions:
- Tell the curious that your scars are a badge of courage (and a summertime fashion statement).
- With a little aluminum foil and some hair barrettes the homing device in your head can pick up cellular phone calls.
- Boast about your free gynecological exam.
- Submit your varied and recurring nightmares to the *X-Files*.

THE SEVEN BASIC TYPES OF ETs
You know 'em, you love 'em, you can live better off without 'em.

As you can't tell a player without a scorecard, you can't tell an extraterrestrial without these Official Alien Trading Cards (collect them before they collect you):

1) Roswells: Reptilian skin, human eyes, named after the famous Roswell alien whose sense of adventure is shadowed only by his poor sense of direction. Partial to sports, shopping malls, and small insects. Favorite pastime: Counting the knotholes in army crates.

2) Grays: Small size, black eyes, the worker class. They are tasked with all the dirty work of abduction, including capture, subjugation, medical examination, implantation, memory suppression, and return—and all this without a pension plan. Hobbies: none. Favorite pastime: Fantasizing about worker revolt.

LOCAL
UNION
#23

3) Ancients: Insectlike, large eyes, upper management, their awkward appearance belies their hyperkinetic powers of shape-shifting and weather prediction. Hobbies: Imagining the destruction of entire galaxies, and then holding back. Favorite pastime: *Sports Illustrated* swimsuit edition.

4) Nordics: Humanlike, athletic build, well-endowed, like Fabio on steroids, this is the race assigned to supervise the takeover of planet Earth—as soon as they finish hair-styling training. They like sports, sex, and hunting (usually in combination). Favorite pastime: Masturbating to Nietzsche.

5) Hybrids: Small, childlike, with fine hair and *Children of the Damned* demeanor (which also describes their spiritual kinship to the Mighty Morphin Power Rangers). Hobbies: Burning the legs off helpless animals with only their right corneas. Favorite pastime: Impersonating *your* child!

6) Reptilians: Snakelike, three-toed, charming carnivores who are fond of small moist areas like your rump. They apparently serve no function other than annoying the other aliens. Favorite pastime: Practicing law.

7) Neonates: Highly intelligent, fetuslike, young Turks with MBAs who carry cellular phones and read *Variety*. Partial to Jacuzzis, milk baths, and cow placentas. Hobbies: Planting stories about the inevitable alien takeover in *TV Guide*. Favorite pastime: Toppling world governments.

THE ALIEN ABDUCTOR'S CHECKLIST

IDENTIFICATION
Is the abductee:
[   ] conscious
[   ] unconscious
[   ] a New Ager

[   ] male
[   ] female
[   ] a fundamentalist preacher

If the abductee is female, is she:
[   ] of childbearing age
[   ] below childbearing age
[   ] of Shirley MacLaine age

If the abductee is male, is he:
[   ] potent
[   ] impotent
[   ] Woody Allen

blood type:
[   ] O+
[   ] A+
[   ] B+
[   ] Cabernet Caucasian

MEDICATION
YES!!

MEDICAL PROCEDURES

Tissue samples:

[ ] skin
[ ] hair
[ ] lymph glands
[ ] will to live

Implant type to be replaced:

[ ] after four years
[ ] after 400,000 sneezes

Memory allocation:

[ ] total temporary removal
[ ] partial temporary removal
[ ] white supremacists

Reproductive:

[ ] sperm collection
[ ] egg fertilization
[ ] fetal extraction
[ ] anal probe (Optional: just for fun)

PSYCHOLOGICAL TESTING

when presented with images of Earth's destruction at the hands of their fellow humans, the abductee:

[ ] weeps uncontrollably
[ ] stares catatonically
[ ] asks for a replay

when shown images of a peaceful and harmonious world under the control of the new alien world government, the abductee:

[ ] cowers in fear
[ ] sighs in awe
[ ] defecates in pants

MESSENGER QUOTIENT

the abductee's potential for absorbing and spreading our message of inevitable conquest and supremacy is:

[ ] good
[ ] fair
[ ] poor
[ ] so poor that return is not necessary

HOW TO APPEAR ON TALK SHOWS

An opportunity to convince a skeptical public of the truth of your experience, or merely an electronic crucifixion for the viewing pleasure of millions.

TV talk shows are risky venues for validating your encounter, considering how easily your appearance could turn into a second rape. Not that the producers of these holeflappers intend to toss you into the waiting jaws of public ridicule like a Christian fed to the lions; it's just that when their competition is transsexual pederasts on death row, you start looking like fresh meat.

The image you present is most important. So, assume that the audience will be predisposed to view you as a stray dog views a public hydrant, and dress with dignity and taste. When the red light above the camera turns on, state your experiences directly and concisely (leaving out inflammatory expletives like "Nazi-loving alien scum!"). When your veracity is questioned, you can choose from among several responses:

— Show them your scars (on those body parts permitted to be seen on national TV).

— Display your medical records and say, "You don't just lose a fetus this size on a two-mile trip to Seven-Eleven in a Volvo—and we *did* look behind the dash!"

— Demonstrate your new telekinetic powers by straightening Geraldo's nose.

— Offer to illustrate the aliens' breeding techniques in the Green Room with Dennis Rodman on a *Sports Illustrated* swimsuit model.

— Beseech the studio audience to relinquished its rampant materialism, work for world peace, and escort you home en masse.

— Connect the dots with the implants on your Xray that spell out the words: Return Postage Guaranteed.

As a spokesperson for the abductee experience, you must lucidly make your case for acceptance, tolerance, and understanding (kindness may be too much to expect from a crowd that enjoys watching mud-wrestling vampires in tutus). Keep in mind that there are two basic types of talk-show audiences: 1) hostile nose-pickers who have problems breeding outside of their own family (with this they have a lot in common with aliens); and 2) supportive and sincere creeps. The second type is almost worse: Smarmy and mealy-minded, they wallow in victim pity and expect you to love them for it.

Whether they mock you with open hostility, or overpower you with a passive-aggressive Telethon-inspired emotional mugging, remember that nonbelievers are really just frightened human beings, so treat their ignorant reactions to your plight with the patience it deserves—then pull out your Uzi and spray the bastards dead!!!

WHY NONABDUCTEES DON'T BELIEVE

The pure and simple truth is rarely pure and never simple.
— Oscar Wilde

The typical nonabductee is firmly convinced that reality is like concrete—solid and immovable. Of course he's convinced, his reality has never been challenged (just wait till he gets probed by four-foot gray Gumbies). But nonabductees are not the world's first nonbelievers. Many people thought Dr. Louis Pasteur's theory of sterilization was a sham. Later they believed that England would rule forever and that man could never fly. Show a caveman a color TV and watch him scream in terror (especially if they're rerunning the *Dukes of Hazzard*).

Some years ago I interviewed author Robert Anton Wilson for a TV documentary I produced called "Borders." During the interview he touched on what I think is the central issue of belief: "Because of our mammalian habits of breaking things down into territories, we all create our own reality-tunnel. . . . If we're born in Dublin, Ireland, we see an Irish-Catholic reality tunnel for our whole lives. If we are born in Moscow we see a Marxist reality tunnel our whole lives. If we're born in Iran we see an Islamic-fundamentalist reality tunnel. If we're born in England and graduate from Cambridge, we see a Cambridge-Agnostic reality tunnel. Getting outside reality tunnels and perceiving the non-verbal, nonsymbolic infinite flux of which we are part is very, very difficult for domesticated primates [humans]. I think it's worth trying, however. The real world is much more exciting and wiggly and alive than all of our stereotyped little reality tunnels put together."

In other words, today's aliens might be tomorrow's noisy neighbors. So, if one of those solipsistic, mentally constipated, pea-brained, tunnel-visioned, evolutionary-challenged nonbees question your veracity—just smile thoughtfully and say nothing—then give out their home address on your next junket.

ALIEN SEX
(No, I don't mean Michael Jackson.)

You may not think your alien abductors care about you, but rest assured that they do. They care about your liver, your kidneys, and most especially, your eggs and sperm. And while an alien's romantic overtures may preclude a candlelight dinner and soft music, their exquisite taste in DNA makes them most attentive to your body. Many abductees report improved health prior to actual alien sexual encounters. The superior alien medical science has mended broken bones, improved eyesight, cured arthritis, and healed wounds. Immortality might finally become ours—if we are willing to bed down with the star-hopping emissaries of love, goodwill, and horniness. These intergalactic cruisers are apparently not as motivated by their love of humankind as they are by their need to breed. The alien's gene stock is thinly stretched, due to centuries of inbreeding more entrenched and traditional than an Ozark wedding. This makes them impatient lovers, forsaking foreplay for a more direct approach: anal probes, ejaculation pumps, and egg extractors.

But just because alien lovers equate sexual intimacy with a quick tune-up, it doesn't mean that they aren't hygienic. Safe sex is always foremost in their minds. The needles and metal probes are sterilized, and the stirrups are always kept shiny and sanitary (and somewhat cold). At times a form-fitting white gooey cushion might envelop your body and lift you up into the blinding examination lights of desire. At other times you'll be totally restrained by the simple use of their telekinetic powers of love. All in all, you'll most likely remain untouched by any of their limbs, but thoroughly defiled by all of their instruments. And after all this they won't even pay for dinner.

HOW TO TELL YOUR FIANCÉE

"Honey, there's something you ought to know. . . . I've done the wild thing on the far side of the moon."

Nothing is more exhilarating than a new love affair, unless it's the rush of fear when you imagine revealing your "little secret" to your future spouse. Sooner or later your betrothed will discover your scoop marks, hear you mutter in your sleep, "No, not the probe!" or find child support requests from Zeta Reticuli. As if relationships weren't hard enough, you now carry the baggage of ongoing abductions, which is a heavier load than infidelity, herpes, or an ex-spouse without a restraining order.

The first step is disclosure—not full disclosure, mind you, but the type of disclosure that is kind, considerate of your fiancée's emotions, and as tactful as an intelligence agent at a congressional UFO investigation.

Begin by revealing little secrets first: your nocturnal gas attacks, your history with the IRS, your penchant for rubber items and small farm animals, your continuing love for your other spouse still living in New Zealand. Then throw in a hint or two: Say, "I have a kid from a prior relationship, but it never comes to visit—alone," or "There's nothing I'd like better than a quiet trip with you—as long as it's in a tour bus with the graduating class of West Point." Sometimes visual clues can help: saucer-shaped cookies, condoms, and diaphragms, just to name a few. Then, when you unload the whole ugly story, the moment of truth will arrive: Will your fiancée stay the course of true love, and stick with you through the terrible adversity of abductions, ridicule, and ostracism—or disappear quicker than a crashed saucer in a military installation?

ABDUCTEE SEX

"Not tonight, dear, I'm having a regression."

Most abductees are so traumatized by their abductions that regular sex is usually out of the question (along with regular eating, regular sleeping, and regular bowel movements). But despite the overwhelming obstacles to human intimacy—even in the most ordinary of circumstances—abductees can have a full and rewarding sex life—even with a partner.

Set the ground rules: Communication with your partner is the first step to breaking down those fears that make achieving orgasm almost as difficult as getting the military to release the dead Roswell alien. By simply telling your partner that you've tried S&M and don't like it, you're off to a good start. (Of course, there are some abductees who have actually enjoyed their breeding sessions with extraterrestrials. And while it is outside the scope of this tome to delve into the varieties of alternative exo-sex—the U.S. postal rules still apply—the author makes no judgment on those who relish the steady, dispassionate gaze of those deep black bug-eyes; the soft sticky touch of an alien's skin; the long steely needle inserted slowly, slowly into your bottom . . . oh, . . . excuse me!)

Set the mood: Blackened windows not only set a romantic mood for the evening, they also prevent tell-tale light from leaking out to the curious lurking (or floating) nearby. Music also helps set the mood (avoid the theme song from *Close Encounters*.) Once you are relaxed and comfortably close, you can slowly begin the process of foreplay. Revealing your erogenous zones to your partner should now be easy: "Just to the left of that triangular red scar." Revealing your fantasies to your partner, however, is unnecessary (just keep those images of gnawing on the raw heart of an alien to yourself, particularly during oral foreplay).

Mission lift-off! Having successfully (if momentarily) eradicated any memories of past abductions, you can now enjoy the pleasure of an intimate encounter. Keep in tune with your partner's rhythm, movement, and breathing (you may, however, want to refrain from thinking about sweat and other sticky bodily fluids to thwart those annoying and unpleasant memory flashbacks). Remember, of course, to play it safe. Condoms should do the trick. And for those truly cautious, a portable Geiger counter.

Postcoital pillow talk: Even if your evening of bliss is just a one-night stand, the truly enlightened partner of an abductee will want to spend some quality time cuddling with you—at least until those unmarked black helicopters start buzzing the bedroom (after that you may be on your own). You know you've struck gold, however, if your lover gently strokes your hair and lovingly rubs your neck without saying, "Ouch" if he or she scrapes a finger on your implant.

HOW TO PICK UP ABDUCTEE CHICKS
Because even abductees get lonely—for humans.

Earth abductee chicks are not necessarily easy (no matter what their abductors say), but they are usually available. And while a night of perimeter walking and high-voltage fence-mending may not be everyone's ideal date, you can discover a world of delight, comfort, and the unexpected from a girl whose previous suitors had all the charm of Dr. Mengele and all the romance of Don Knotts.

Where to find abductee chicks: At support groups, New Age seminars, organic food markets, and the offices of cosmetic surgeons.

Putting her at ease: Remember, abductee chicks have gone through physical pain, long-term mental anguish, lingering bouts of depression, and constant feelings of worthlessness and humiliation; so telling your story about how your last girlfriend stole your CD collection won't get you any sympathy. For starters, look deep into her eyes, and with a soothing, soft voice say, "I know the pain you've been through." This will make her see you as a sincere and caring solicitor on your first date. What you don't want to do is: recommend a great shrink, ask to see her scars, or say, "You must know some really wild positions!"

Winning her heart: The way to an abductee's heart is through her frontal lobes: Convince her not only of your belief in UFOs and aliens, but also your extensive knowledge of government conspiracies, Russian aerospace, alternate worlds, and that special hiding place you discovered behind Stonehenge. Then, as the sandalwood incense burns, as Frank Black plays in the background, caress her aura and watch her crystals fall.

Keeping her happy: Believe what she says, and watch what she does. If you're not able to deal with her 4 A.M. bouts of anxiety, astral projection, and *I Ching* binges, then you should probably move in with a horticulturist. Resist the temptation to be jealous over her extraterrestrial love life. After all, she doesn't ask you about your obsessive affair with the calendar girl from the *Weekly World News*. And remember, if it wasn't for her, you'd still be hanging with the raincoat crowd in your local occult bookstore.

HOW TO BREAK UP WITH YOUR ABDUCTEE BOYFRIEND
Hit the asteroid belt, Jack!

Why you have to split: Nothing is more stressful than being abducted—unless it's trying to end a relationship with your abductee boyfriend. Maybe you've grown tired of rubbing your hand over his scars to convince him that they're real; perhaps you harbor lingering doubts about all those late-night encounters; or maybe you stockpile serious suspicions about his female friends at group counseling. (How can you—someone who has never seen a UFO, let alone any of the seven basic alien types—compete with a fellow abductee? Even if she is a fifty-five-year-old overweight housemother of ten?)

Whatever the specifics, the cause of any abductee relationship breakup is always centered on belief—he doesn't believe that you believe that he believes you when you say that you believe him. No matter how many times you assure him, there will always be that glint of mistrust in his eyes—a glint that sometimes ignites into full-fledged paranoia. And while you may be willing to put up with his accusations (you're only humoring him, you've already booked him a room at the Happyview Health Clinic, you laugh during the movie *Communion*); you certainly shouldn't tolerate giving up any more of your eggs. (So what if your kid turns out looking like Fabio with grasshopper eyes?)

How to become just friends: Nobody likes to be made fun of—especially abductees (just check out the letters section in *The Official Alien Abductee's Handbook, Volume Two*). In no case should you give your former abductee boyfriend the impression that you will talk about him after the split (this will give you a hefty lead time to write your own book way in advance of his). In the meantime, tell him that even though you can't possibly imagine a life without bedroom surveillance monitors, hypno-regression tapes, or sympathy scoop marks, it has become impossible to deal with your feelings of rejection—which he will interpret as jealousy. Let him. Just smile sweetly as you pack your body cream, Band-Aids, Budd Hopkins books, and other items of sentiment, and tell him you'll still be friends; and that you will always remember the way he starts the microwave when he sneezes.

ABDUCTEE PERSONALS
For those in search of true love—restraint free.

KEY TO ABBREVIATIONS:
S = Single
D = Divorced
A = Abducted
AA = Abducted more than once
AAA = Abducted more than once and consequently an alcoholic
AAAAAA = Abducted more than once and consequently an alcoholic but still a member of the Automobile Association of America
M = Male
F = Female
H = Hybrid
URH = Undergoing regressive hypnosis
UPI = Undergoing progressive insanity

WOMEN SEEKING MEN

SAAF intelligent, pretty, with a sense of cosmic unity, in search of large bodyguard with guns—lots of them!

Thirty-two-year-old SAF lonely and confused in search of SAAM for guidance, care, and bandages. Must like camping, biking, and hiding in steel-reinforced underground bunkers where they can't find me again!

In search of financially well-endowed married AM who would love to abduct this nineteen-year-old SF with large chest, long legs, and full, pouting lips. Call me and my friends, but first please mention that you are not a police officer.

Voluptuous DAAF, forty-one, with two AA kids seeking S or DM (A or AA not important) who loves good food, fine wine, and earth-bound sports. Must own car, have large bank account, high cholesterol, and a weak heart.

Slender, pretty, thirty-four-year-old SAAF who is URH looking for experienced and secure SAAM who is also URH. You must be able to match neurosis with denial, and emotional unavailability with chemical dependency. Medical insurance a plus.

MEN SEEKING WOMEN

Tall, dark, adventurous SAAM in love with life seeking SF for instruction, veneration, and desecration on the altar of my ET friends. Let's share and care together!

Successful SAF businessman would love to form a long-term relationship with an insomniac nurse who loves cuddling, cooking, and bedside shotgun riding.

Boisterous, bawdy SMH seeking SF for spiritual surfing on the intergalactic Internet of interspecies breeding. Object: insemination.

Cantankerous, crotchety, elderly retired DM wants SAAF to exchange experiences, body massages, bodily fluids, and, eventually, bodies.

SAAM seeking to join forces with SAAF and exploit our expanded consciousness, psychic talent, and publishing power. Object: market share domination. (Have my abductor call your abductor.)

WOMEN SEEKING WOMEN

AAF, on the verge of Harmonic Convergence, wishes to merge with a knowing, passionate, and tolerant entity. Religion, race, and species not important.

Worried, empathic Vegan F seeking friendly AA who can awaken my chakras. Bring your own wok.

Aggressive, erotic, and full-figured UPI seeks fearless AA for sexy midnight abductions. No butches, nuns, president's wives, or CIA operatives. Shaved head a plus!

MEN SEEKING MEN

Secure professional Papa Bear, AAA, hairy all over, looking for cute, clean non-A for instruction in cosmic love, imported leather, and terrestrial dominance.

Body by Nautilus, mind by Freud. Looking for a muscular AA to work out together in my home gym: weights, racquetball, and astral body rubs. Sinewy muscle tone and scoop marks a must!

Transplanted Eurasian AA, attractive and refined, seeks A or AA companion for Broadway, opera, concerts, or just a simple night home channeling Judy Garland.

HOW TO AVOID BEING ABDUCTED

Tips, tricks, and desperate ruses.

You can try prayers, hexes, bug repellent, garlands of garlic, and that autographed photo of Richard Nixon, but they won't ward off abductions. There may be no sure deterrent, but the following suggestions could prove useful, especially if being abducted is as appealing to you as being the test subject in a CPR class run by Dr. Kevorkian.

1: SEEK SANCTUARY.

Unlike federal agents, the Mossad, and your mom, there are certain places aliens can't—or won't—go. Areas that can guarantee you safety from snatching include:

1) Gambling casinos run by Native Americans.
2) Bathroom stalls in the New York City subway.
3) The Customer Complaint Department of Macy's.
4) Any Department of Motor Vehicles office.
5) Yanni concerts.

2: BECOME A FAUX HUMAN.

This will have those aliens turning their noses (and gills) up at you. No entity wants an imitation when they can get the real thing. Successful covers include:

White rap groups
Conservative Democrats
Dick Clark
Talk show hosts
All Republicans
Elvis imitators

VCR repairmen
Internet pimps
Telephone company solicitors
Anyone on infomercials
People with full-body tattoos (The aliens' scanners can't read them, then they have to call the manager, then you have to wait while everyone behind you in line gets real annoyed.)

A must to avoid:
Seventh-Day Adventists *(How do you think they hide from us?)*

3: BECOME A UFO INVESTIGATOR.
This has one of the highest degrees of success, for no known competent UFO investigators have ever been abducted (no matter how hard they've tried). And no known abductees have ever found Zeta Reticuli on a map (let alone that shortcut route where they lost two hours).

#4: WHEN ALL ELSE FAILS—get a vasectomy or get your tubes tied! It may not totally stop the abductions, but it sure will piss off those aliens when they get you under the knife!

NEAR-DEATH EXPERIENCES AND ALIEN ABDUCTIONS

In one you are dying, in the other you wish you were.

A lot has been written about near-death experiences. (A lot has also been written about the G-spot, but I've yet to find it.) Apparently, millions have experienced the process of dying and have returned to tell about it: how they floated up and out of their bodies toward a bright shining white light where they encountered all-powerful beings who enveloped them with compassion and love when they were suddenly returned back into their bodies and left with both a sense of loss and revitalization. By now you can see several similarities between near-death experiences and alien abductions:

- The bright white light that either signals a loving welcoming or a triumphant catch of the day

- Encounters with beings who are either dear departed relatives, or hideous, sadistic torturers who look like your uncle Fred

- An immersion in a self-examination of profound spiritual insights, or a clinical forced-physical examination of profound and insidious intrusion

- A gentle descent back into your body, or a crash-landing in a deserted cow field miles from any public transportation or reasonable car service

- The resulting feelings of loss, excitement, and savoring the second-to-second preciousness that is daily life, or the resulting feelings of anger, pain, and humiliation while waiting in dread for the next occurrence

THE LIGHTER SIDE OF ALIEN ABDUCTIONS

No Pain, No Enlightenment.

While most abductees view their abductions as painful, humiliating, and just darn inconvenient, some have successfully transcended the initial trauma, turning it into a positive growth experience that has helped them lead full and productive lives (while still leaving enough time for special appearances at New Age seminars). Many abductees who undergo this conversion have become ecological advocates, working for a cleaner environment and a better life for all of Earth's creatures. This is probably the best response to an alien abduction, letting the aliens know that we mean to clean up our act, and may prevent them from treating our planet like we have for centuries—like one giant trash can.

This transformative, mystical experience seems to be rooted in a concept as ancient as alchemy, but as trendy as high-top sneakers. The Gaia concept assumes that Earth is a living, conscious entity and that UFOs and aliens are a manifestation of Earth's consciousness, which is designed to elevate us poor, stupid humans to a higher level of understanding when everything mysterious will now be made clear—including cow mutilations and Partridge Family revivals.

The transformed abductee can relax in the knowledge that all living creatures are one, and that when the aliens scrape your eggs and your sperm they are taking a piece from themselves as much as they are from you. And even though cosmic consciousness may come at the price of body scars and fetal extraction, enlightenment has never come easy—just ask Jesus on your next trip.

ALIEN ABDUCTION OF CHILDREN

Unfortunately it happens. And if you think I'm going to make a joke about it you can stop reading right now. You're probably the type who thinks *America's Most Wanted* is a game show and calls concentration camps health spas.

ALIEN ABDUCTEE NURSERY RHYMES

The aliens are indoctrinating our children! These insidious poems were found on the bottom of Big Bird's cage and indisputably prove that the aliens not only plan to capture the minds of the young, but Public Broadcasting as well (how else do you explain Barney?).

Humpty Dumpty sat on a wall.
Humpty Dumpty had a great fall.
All the King's horses, and all the King's men,
Sealed the area; gathered and locked up all the pieces;
intimidated, harassed, and threatened all witnesses;
and will admit nothing 'til who knows when.

Little Miss Cegeny
Sat on her settee
Drinking a fine Bordeaux.
When a sudden bright light
Caused her great fright
And months later she started to show.

Jack and Jill went up the hill
To catch some falling stars.
When Jill reappeared,
it caused Jack a fear,
'cause her body was covered in scars.

Richard E. Horner
Sat in the corner
Reciting official denials.
When an alien landed
he found himself branded,
which confused him just for a while.

Hey diddle diddle
I'll tell you a riddle
A saucer flew over the moon.
It landed in Roswell
Where army personnel
called it a weather balloon.

STAGING
All the universe is a stage, and you're on permanent audition.

No one is certain, but it is thought that aliens are continually testing abductees to discover specific human traits they themselves lack: compassion, humor, desire, and guilt, just to mention a few. To this end they have produced a kind of intergalactic community theater, devised to elicit our responses to staged phenomena—staged for them, but all too real for us.

These elaborate staging scenarios can be thought of as the cosmic casting couch where humans are put through intense scenes: forced seductions with the opposite sex, captures by giant satanic figures, even terrorist actions by midget-size alien soldiers. The scenarios are short, but the drama is intense, if somewhat amateurish—like a bad Hollywood movie with no second act. The aliens' sense of catharsis is limited to the Pavlovian School of Triggered Response, an extreme form of method acting that's like being enclosed in a torture chamber while bleachers full of season ticket holders rate the delivery of your agonized screams. You might find yourself, for example, strapped to the wing of a old B-29 plane as it bursts into flames: the triggered response—fear. Or you might be driving down the street when a toddler on a tricycle juts in front of you and you mow the kid down: the triggered response—guilt (unless, of course, it's one of those hybrid toddlers).

In each case, abductees report discovering aliens acting opposite them, dressed almost appropriately for the "roles." The Andy Hardy anthem, "Hey, kids, let's put on a show!" becomes the alien chant, "Hey, comrades, look at those primate specimens twitch!" And where alien science and art meet, human psychotherapy will take years to repair. There seems to be no sense in resisting either; you'll just be recast and put on double matinees.

So when you discover yourself on stage, acting a scene from your own personal *Oedipus Rex* to the delight of hundreds of intergalactic popcorn-chewing Gumbies, keep in mind one comforting thought: at least you're not working for Andrew Lloyd Webber!

MEDIA DISPLAY
Where your home planet hosts the Galactic Demolition Derby.

Many alien recreational activities take place around a customized home entertainment center so technologically advanced it makes satellite-delivered TV look like C-SPAN Shadow Puppet Theater. With a giant-size TV screen, supersurround sound, and a captive audience—you—the aliens have forgotten nothing, including the admission price—again, you. The purpose would seem to be indoctrination on an order not seen since the New Coke campaign. To make you more willing to undergo their reproduction operations, the aliens have produced a mini-series about Earth where chaos reigns, pollution is king, and its subjects (guess who) are dead.

First you are led into a roped-off area inside a large room where you stand with other naked humans (your genitalia are your ticket stub). Next you are shown horrific scenes of Earth's destruction at the hands of reckless humans (in other words, just about any segment from CNN). Then, these interplanetary Oliver Stones follow this cautionary tale with a contrasting sequel of idyllic scenes of Earth (warm and green living pastures, floating puffy clouds, humans and aliens living together in harmony). All of this takes place after alien intervention and eventual rule (in other words, EuroDisney without the French).

What is actually behind the aliens' intervention plan is their hyperspace version of a twelve-step program:

Step 1: Shame and humiliate you until you admit that you are personally responsible for decades of war, exploitation, slavery, pollution, and bad hair weaves.

Step 2: Subjugate and imprison you until you feel a dependency with them not felt since your ex left with the car and bank account.

Step 3: Counsel and console you with utopian visions of the future with your alien comrades (you're the one with the dog collar).

Step 4: Telepathically coerce you into seeking their forgiveness for the collective sins of humanity while they extract your egg and sperm with instruments more sterile than a postal worker's imagination.

Step 5: Secure your loyalty and devotion with promises of a better tomorrow and a controlling implant in your brain.

Step 6: Form a strong bond between you and your personal alien mentor through cosmic understanding, interspecies communication, and a blinding white light so strong you just have to grab hold of something.

Step 7: Initiate deep inside you an uncontrollable desire for family reunions every month at the Zeta Reticuli feeding farm.

Step 8: Stop those bad habits of yours like: greed, aggression, envy, and thinking of yourself as a free agent.

Step 9: Learn to recruit others to the alien cause through environmental activism, spiritual prostelization, and home-baked psychotropic mushrooms.

Step 10: Inspire you to write *The Official Alien Abductee's Handbook.*

Step 11: Instruct you how to contort yourself into yoga positions that take the shape of DNA molecules.

Step 12: Did they ever mention that they love you?

MINDSCAN
A mind is a terrible thing to taste.

Part of the alien abduction plan seems to include a rather extreme version of Truth or Dare: They scan your mind for the truth and dare you to stop them. Mindscan occurs when one of the aliens (usually the "taller, swarthier" one) leans his fat bug-eyed face only inches away from you while you lay prone and restrained. This allows "him" closer access to your cranium, and permits him to scan your mind and check your rapidly increasing gray hairs.

During Mindscan your entire memory is plumbed, including your deepest fears and most hidden secrets (also including your preference for latex articles and knotted nylons). The alien may attempt to calm you by telling you, telepathically, how "special" or "important" you are to it—the intergalactic equivalent of "I'm certain I tested negative." Several abductees report a romantic or sexual quality during Mindscan. The alien may even induce rapid sexual arousal followed by involuntary orgasm (the kind the author used to get at age twelve while reading *National Geographic*).

The purpose of Mindscan is unknown. Perhaps the aliens are amused by our fantasies and easily stimulated by our easily stimulated erogenous zones. Maybe they see themselves as the Masters and Johnson of Alpha Centuri and are cataloging our sexual responses as part of a how-to book on human mating. Then again, they could just be extraterrestrial swingers out cruising some easily preyed-on prey.

SCREEN MEMORY
Where an active imagination is your only salvation.

Like a recipient of Publishers Clearinghouse junk mail, you may have already been abducted and not even know it! In fact, your mind is probably playing guard dog right now, replacing the gory details of your abduction with a substitute memory as phony as a government denial. Figuring you'd rather not remember being covered in green slime while examined rectally, your brain conveniently invents a scenario of falling in a puddle with a minor case of hemorrhoids. Or, by camouflaging your encounter with the bug-eyed ones, you instead recall a late evening's conference with some gregarious owls (the fact that you can't remember exactly how you collared those red scars only means the discussion got a little heated.)

Should you decide to undergo regressive hypnosis and actually recover those long-buried, pleasant memories of abuse and subjugation, you'd do well to remember the fate of those who suffered the ill effects of a total recall, and arm yourself with a sufficient supply of ready-to-wear screen memories:

Here are the latest screen memories for the new fall season:
• Fly-fishing with circus midgets
• A tattoo session with Native American Hell's Angels
• An appointment with your proctologist, the grasshopper.

HYPNOTIC REGRESSION
A walk through memory lane, or a stroll down the garden path?

So you think you've been abducted, but can't tell for sure? Take a session with your local hypnotist. There are several who now specialize in abductions. And, unlike ambulance-chasing lawyers, they actually care about you; many offer their services for free. The only price is that of recovering long-suppressed abduction episodes where you relive unfathomable fear, unbearable pain, and unending humiliation. A small price to pay for discovering your new identity—Victim.

First, see if you display any of the classic signs of abduction: missing time, recurring strange dreams, scoop marks, Post-it notes with "To be picked up later" stuck on your nipples. If you discover any of these symptoms—get thee to a therapist!

Choosing your therapist is almost as important as choosing the right shade of scar-covering powder. Your therapist should be experienced in handling cases of human abduction (beware of off-planet medical licenses), and should respect your desire not to have your session videotaped and included on a *Hard Copy* episode called "Skywatching Kooks." Because you want to be certain of your abduction, beware also of therapists who ask leading questions, like: "Try to recall the small gray creature with the long silver needle . . . Remember how it felt as it was inserted."

A typical session begins with the hypno-therapist placing you in a relaxed position and asking you to breathe deeply. You'll then be put in a trance and be guided to remember an incident from your past. Whether it is a scene from early childhood or an episode from last week, what is recalled is usually traumatic and terrifying, turning remembering into the psychic equivalent of dirt-biking across landminds. Because the purpose of therapy is to relieve your fear and integrate your experience (not trigger endless flashbacks sandwiched between feelings of unjustified persecution) the therapist should validate your feelings and help you distance yourself from them. If your therapist is skillful, compassionate, and understanding, the healing process should take no more than two to six sessions; if not, you may consider either marrying your therapist, or murdering him.

POSTABDUCTION SYNDROME

Some cures for what you feel like the morning after, and the morning after, and the morning after . . .

THE SYMPTOMS:

Fear of being alone.

Fear of doctors' offices.

Panic attacks.

Aversions to animals with big eyes.

Baby avoidance.

THE CURES:

Massage therapy with the Turbo-Vibrator.

Chanting the mantra "Malpractice" with a lawyer by your side.

Owning a life-size doll of Arnie the Alien with the easily squashable head.

Velvet painting classes.

Moving to a retirement home.

FALSE-MEMORY SYNDROME
The memory you recover may be the one you never had.

Sure, your therapist is kind, thoughtful, and understanding. He could also be suggestive, domineering, and controlling. And while he may be helping you integrate your traumatic feelings from alien abuse, in fact that trauma may be just a drama.

Like the Salem witch trials and the McCarthy Communist hunts, repressed memories of abuse could be as false as a politician's election vow. As much as 25 percent of so-called repressed memories are just not true, according to Dr. Elizabeth Loftus. It has gotten so bad that some patients who previously reported memories of childhood abuse are now suing their eager-to-publish-and-get-on-*Oprah* therapists. These therapists engage in wildly suggestive methods in order to elicit these specific memories, and cash in on a popular trend—even though their documentation is as scarce as a bag of pork rinds in a fundamentalist mosque.

Alien abductees face a double bind. Being without empirical evidence of their own abduction, they are not only disbelieved by the public, but now also manipulated by erstwhile sympathetic just-as-eager-to-publish-and-get-on-*Geraldo* therapists.

So be careful. Your recovered memory may be about as reliable as a fishnet condom. To be sure your therapist is not coaxing, suggesting, or implanting false memories of abduction, check for these tell-tale signs:

DOES YOUR THERAPIST:

- Provide you with a multiple-choice checklist of the top ten favorite abduction scenarios?

- Include on his patient consent form a clause assigning him your life story (including, but not limited to, all of your past lives)?

- Conceal *Hard Copy* reporters behind his couch?

- Invite you to imagine being strapped on a table inside a large spaceship as he slips on a rubber glove?

Finally, ask yourself this: Are you sure you've really been abducted? Do you really want to know? For peace of mind and serenity of spirit, you may need to remember only the following: Ignorance is bliss, Prozac is cheap.

HAVE YOU BEEN ABDUCTED?

Quiz #2

1) ON YOUR BODY THERE ARE:
   a) Hickeys from your lover
   b) Tattoos from your past
   c) Scoop marks from your new owners

2) YOU NATURALLY GRAVITATE TOWARD PEOPLE WHO ARE:
   a) Fluent in the culinary arts and have traveled nationally
   b) Fluent in several languages and have traveled internationally
   c) Fluent in astrology and have vacationed with you in past lives

3) WHEN YOU AWAKE IN THE MORNING YOU FIND:
   a) A smile on your face and a song in your heart
   b) Wax in your ears and sleep in your eyes
   c) Mud on your feet and blood in your stool

CONSPIRACIES À GO-GO

Just because you're paranoid doesn't mean there aren't hundreds of plausible reasons why you've been targeted by aliens and terrestrials alike.

The conspiracy theories surrounding UFOs and aliens make the JFK assassination seem like a walk in Dealey Plaza. To simplify things, one can break the controversy within the UFO community into two camps: those who believe the government is withholding information about UFOs and aliens, and those who think the government is deliberately leaking disinformation about UFOs and aliens. (Of course, both these camps assume that the government acts in consort, while we all know that if one branch of the government ever knew what the other branch was doing, it would surely be an accident of even greater mystery than the authorship of the Majestic 12 report.)

Here are several selected conspiracies. Choose one, choose many, try them on for size, but don't get too wrapped up in any one of them. Conspiracies are like religions, to be embraced for comfort in time of need, but not to be trusted for too long.

• Bob Barry, director of the twentieth-century UFO bureau at Colinswood, New Jersey, states that the movie *Close Encounters of the Third Kind* was part of a government plan to condition the public to accept the existence of UFOs and aliens. If so, was it also the government who supplied cocaine to producer Julia Phillips?

• Founding CIA officer (and father of one of the members of the rock band The Police) Miles Copeland confirmed that the agency used UFO mythology in a disinformation campaign. In his example, top-secret research efforts were covered up by Ufology to disinform the Chinese government. This is probably why, during the band's Asian tour, Sting seemed to be sending cryptic signals with his bass frets.

• Some hyperactive (read "paranoid") Ufologists claim that the aliens have formed a pact with the U.S. government and that an eventual alien nation will soon rise to power. According to these researchers, an ultra-top secret constitution was signed by both parties in which all citizens will be monitored during waking hours and be harvested for genetic interbreeding during the night—leaving any remaining time for extracurricular activities sanctioned only by the new alien government. These include: synchronized protein chewing, sperm shuffleboard, genetic roulette, and Barney worshiping.

*** **News Flash:** It seems the aliens, like all good political beings, are hedging their bets. Other top-secret constitutions have recently emerged, signed by different countries. The new alien constitution of Jamaica will include a provision that would make it mandatory to smoke big spliffs of marijuana rolled in the shape of the Bermuda Triangle. In Asia, the new alien government would make it a crime punishable by death to sing in a frequency higher than 128Mhz. Saudi Arabia's new alien-run government allows women to have more than one husband—as long as their husbands have huge bug-eyes and copulate in laboratories.

PSY-OPS AND PC BASHING
(Just when you thought it was safe to believe Oliver Stone . . .)

As any true conspiracy buff will tell you, the ultimate conspiracy theory states that the government in fact uses conspiracy theories to maintain its control on us. These Psychological Operations ("Psy-ops") create confusion among the population during times of national tensions—like war, elections, and IRS filings. The proof (according to film director Alex Cox in *UFO Magazine*, Volume 10, #1, 1995), is the following: from the '40s through the '60s all major reports on UFOs and alien intelligence have come from our own native alien intelligence—the U.S. military; the official U.S. Air Force's investigation into UFOs was directed by Major General Charles P. Cabell (who, along with Alan Dulles and CIA Plans Director Richard Bissel, was fired after the Bay of Pigs party) a covert operations specialist who could have used the UFO controversy as a nifty cover for special "black operations"; Cabell was also later targeted by New Orleans district attorney Jim Garrison for the JFK murder, but never prosecuted; the "crashed UFO" rumor in Pennsylvania in 1965 was a psy-op sired to cloak recovery of the crashed Soviet *Kosmos-96* Venus probe; billions of dollars from the U.S. military's secret program allowance are spent on the Groom Lake base in Nevada, a popular spot for alien-watchers who believe that alien spacecraft are tested there regularly.

The fact that the U.S. Air Force has continually spent much of its time debunking UFO sightings and such only adds fuel to Cox's fire: "Cabell's three Air Force Intelligence projects, Blue Book, Sign, and Grudge, are still cited as evidence by Ufologists convinced the Air Force is 'covering up.' To me the existence of not one but three different Air Force investigations, potentially with three different explanations for the same event, and three different sets of conclusions—all of them potentially false—suggests a classic intelligence-constructed 'hall of mirrors' in which the 'real' truth can be hidden behind several veils from foreign spies, and, more importantly [sic], from domestic watchdogs."

True or what? In one sense Cox's argument echoes the Hungarian government's 1954 announcement (here retold by John Spencer from the *UFO Encyclopedia*) that "UFOs do . . . not exist because all flying saucer reports originate . . . in the bourgeois countries, where they were invented by the capitalist warmongers with a view to drawing the people's attention away from their economic difficulties." Again, I feel too much credit is given to the military intelligence (another oxymoron) that could mastermind such lavish schemes, but who knows? Most people will do anything for a buck, and the U.S. military so far has received the lion's share (kickbacks from their friends in the defense industry only sweetens their pot).

A final conspiracy theory on this matter involves Alex Cox's own filmmaking turn to the political after his sci-fi-flavored debut film *Repo Man*. Could this be another piece of the long and expensive campaign to disinform the American public? Or perhaps Mr. Cox is himself an alien double agent, awaiting the financing to shoot his grand opus *Close Encounters of the Third World*, a film where the downtrodden masses arise and overtake their oppressors—assisted by their liberators from Zeta Reticuli.

MIND CONTROL, AMERICAN STYLE

*Q: How many ex-Nazi scientists does it take to change
   a lightbulb?*

*A: In the interest of national security, that information is
   strictly classified, and besides, who told you it was a lightbulb?*

Just when you thought it was safe to believe your own mind . . .

So you thought the Cold War was over? The same was said
about bellbottoms, sideburns, and racial hatred. Although the
Soviet Union collapsed under the weight of its weapons expendi-
tures, the U.S. military-industrial complex shows no signs of
slowing down—particularly in the arena of intelligence research.
If declassified government documents are any indication, the
CIA, NSA, NIMH, and DARPA have all played with mind control research—with results startlingly similar to UFO abductions.

In the late 1940s the CIA tinkered with narcohypnosis, where a
"test subject" was hypnotized after being administered sedatives
or a combination of sedatives and amphetamines (the classic
"goofball" drug combo that did in John Belushi and many over-
the-top rock stars). The point, besides having a laugh at your
subject's expense, was to develop a truth serum, something handy
for agents in the field (along with their ballpoint poison pellets
and wristwatch detonators).

During the start of the Cold War, these methods were expanded
into the CIA's Project Paperclip, which imported over six hundred top Nazi scientists and set them loose on the minds of
unsuspecting Americans (now you know how commercial TV was
perfected). Paperclip eventually became the notorious MK-

ULTRA. Some declassified U.S. government documents show that, under the tutelage of the CIA, unwitting U.S. citizens were dosed with LSD while a CIA operative sat on a portable toilet, sipping martinis and watching the fun unfold behind two-way mirrors ("See all that you can see, in the Arrr-my!").

But our super-spy scientists did not stop at Electric Kool-Aid Rancid Tests to perfect their mind-control experiments. Other techniques were used besides hypnosis and drugs: microwaves, religious cults, and sensory deprivation. (What's most surprising is the efficiency of a government agency: With one project they were able to create a Las Vegas act, make a profit in shipment, cook a quick hot meal, market incense, and produce Barney videos—the last two are interchangeable).

Hold on, here's where the implants so common among UFO abductions now enter. By his own account, ex-CIA official Vincent Marchetti boasted about how his agency devised a surveillance device by inserting a radio implant inside a cat's cranium (presumably a suitable feline wrangler was always nearby for debriefing and catnipping). Marchetti never mentions limiting the research to animals, although in his mind humans probably fall into that category as well. Neurophysiologist Dr. John C. Lilly twice halted ground-breaking experiments when U.S. intelligence agencies wanted him to direct his brain research into the area of mind control. And, in a 1988 *Los Angeles Times* article, whistle-blower Rex Niles (a witness in a defense subcontractor kickback scheme) was reportedly harassed by microwave transmissions outside his house and a radioactive disk underneath the dash of his car. ("A new feature in your Toyota—Cruise Missile Control!") Niles's sister (also a witness) was buzzed by helicopters circling her home, and when Niles walked near a friend's computer, it went haywire! The similarities are mounting, but does this really indicate that U.S. Intelligence agents are using the mythology of UFOs to cover their nefarious mind control experiments?

Several books on mind control document cases where a screen memory is implanted in the subject's mind to cover up the actual clandestine indoctrination. (Also a handy trick should an "agent" be caught in the field—hypnosis would reveal only the screen memory planted there, which goes a long way in explaining Ronald Reagan's presidency.) Author Martin Cannon reported the story of an abductee who recognized the voice of a friend during her abduction—a friend employed by the CIA. I personally have heard abductee stories where they recalled uniformed military personnel present at their abductions alongside the aliens.

The theory of UFO abductions as a cover for secret mind-control experiments has been kicking around for a short time now. Some see the military using UFO mythology to conceal their future offensives as an invasion from extra-terrestrials. ("Colonel Hussein, we're being attacked!" "Mobilize the troops!" "By UFOs, Colonel!" "Pray to Allah!") So, those brain implants bestowed on you by your friendly grays may actually be remote mind-control devices operated by intelligence agents under deep cover with technology not found in Radio Shack—or Zeta Reticuli. "And now, Mr. Bond, it's time for your fertilization experiment."

A MALE ALIEN ABDUCTEE'S DIARY

Woke up this morning after a night without incident, I believe (must remember to check the video recording). Experiencing an out-of-body hair day, and thinking of tattoos again—a repeating type of design, something like this:

Never much liked mornings. Waking up with missing pieces of time clipped away from my mind like a Penthouse *magazine in the Oral Roberts Library. One memory they haven't touched is when I was six and lost a tooth, but the tooth fairy never left me any money—she just ripped my tooth right out of my mouth. I want it back—bring me my tooth back, you thieving whore!!!*

Maybe those aliens are practicing an advanced form of voodoo with human body parts. Just thinking of all those fetuses in test tubes, resting in row after row like a Dachshund egg hatchery, I fear these "children" of mine are more like my doubles, existing apart from me, living lives of inexplicable alien-ness while imitating the way I groan at "pro-life" TV commercials and ringing up astronomical bills on my credit cards.

Thinking of starting my own religion: The Church of the Defiant Abductee. Our main religious icon will be a blazing-white statue of me gazing up at the sky with my middle finger raised.

I hate the way the deli man looks at me when he rings my order. This vegetarianism is getting very inconvenient, but the thought of any type of animal flesh passing through my lips is about as appealing as sucking on a dead rat from the tailpipe of an oil truck.

Another job interview, but they always end the same—as soon as I step inside the interviewer's office, his computer crashes.

. . . I was right. First thing the guy does is ask me if want a saucer with my coffee. I admit I barked back at him, somewhat paranoid, "What do you mean by that? Trying to be funny?" I never did finish my coffee.

Should I call Celeste today? She's really nice, and cute, but her curiosity in my abductions is verging on the morbid. Yesterday she asked if she could take skin rubbings of my scars for a painting she's making. I don't mind hanging in an art gallery, but I'd rather it not be of my genitalia, even if she enlarges them.

I could meet up with Remy. She seems to like me, but I wonder if I'd have a better chance if I drop the news before or not. The chicks who get turned on at the first mention of my abductions are the ones I'd rather not see more of. I only wind up at some New Age "party" with them which later turns into an evening of channeling, with me as the pay-per-view special.

The professional chicks don't immediately react poorly. They only bong me a couple of times, then slip me the name of a "really good shrink" on Park Avenue.

Another call from the talk show producer. I'll murder my therapist for introducing us. Hanging out with other abductees is one thing, but being sacrificed on the electronic altar is not my idea of therapy. I tell her that when they book an actual living ET on their show, I'll be the guest who'll throw the first blow.

If only my parents hadn't raised me Catholic. Instead of fighting feelings of guilt, fear, and betrayal, I'd be heading an anti-ET militia with shotguns, Uzis, and surface-to-air missiles. If we capture any alive, we'd perform our own medical experiments on them, extract our pound of flesh, so to speak. And if they can't be caught alive, then let the Star Wars begin. 'Cause if you can't scoop 'em, nuke 'em.

I called Peter from my support group and talked longer than I wanted. He claimed to have empowered himself by "offering the gift of forgiveness" to the ETs. I suggested a gift that comes from the end of my shotgun. We have to stop blaming ourselves for being abducted and start an armed resistance. I told Peter I'm contacting my lawyer about helping our group bring a class action suit against the ETs. We'll be sure to include damage for physical and psychological harm, therapists and lawyer's fees, and purchases of Bud Hopkins books.

Bedtime, and this time I'm sleeping on the couch. Tethered to the legs of the couch, clasping my laser zap light, high-frequency audio alarm, and .45 caliber, I await either another night of terror, struggle, subjugation, and unremitting pain—or I'll lay awake all night wondering why they didn't come.

A FEMALE ALIEN ABDUCTEE'S DIARY

The air is so fresh this morning I almost forget I'm still being stalked until I see the muddy footprints on the bedsheet. Why do they always visit after I do the laundry?

My outfit is already picked from last night so I can spend more time on makeup. Cover Girl's Tawny works best over scoop marks, but nothing can help my spreading ass.

A squirrel paid me a visit at breakfast. The little fellow crawled right onto the table when I had a memory flashback. The hideous, hateful aliens had me immobilized and oh, how I wanted to strike back! After this brief flashback, I buried the furry creature next to the others. The vegetable garden should be bursting this spring!

The men in the street hoot and whistle at me, but today I'm wearing my Walkman, so I reverse the headphone polarity and zap them into silence! All of this unwanted attention from creatures I don't want to know (except for Ramon who still doesn't notice me—and I'm unsure if I should try to strike up a conversation with him. Would mentioning my "secret" arouse his protective empathy or scare him off like a baby puppy? I can't dwell on this anymore today, as I told my therapist: It's not the men in my life, it's the life in my men, and I'm just too scared to discover what kind of life may be lurking in there. If it's an egotistical pig who wants to be mothered, I can handle that. But if it's one of them in male clothing, I'd be happier in a bathtub full of cold dishwater.)

Charles, my first client of the day, was resoundingly rude. He just doesn't get it. You can't put an African violet next to agate crystal and expect positive growth results—that only works with Irish ferns.

Healing plants for the city is even more stressful. The paperwork alone makes me long for the country where all the paper is still in the trees. I worked with a team to disentangle a frightened rhododendron from the mayor's windowsill. It took a lot of time, love, and distilled water, but we managed to coax it back to safety (after first getting the mayor's promise not to cut the city's park budget).

I went home early, but felt such an overwhelming fear, a sense of being watched, like an unseen presence in the woodwork and behind the blinds was waiting for me. I spent the rest of the day cleaning, sweeping, and scrubbing, until I would have had to start all over again and so I put on that tight black skirt and called Bobby and asked him to take me to the most crowded nightclub we could find, preferably with no windows or skylights.

My fear of intimacy really rattles Bobby. I know it's frustrating for him, but if he'd stop thinking of himself for just one second, he might notice I have a few scars too—and not just emotional ones. At the bar he moved his hand up my skirt. And although some might see it as an overreaction, I thought my only alternative was kicking him off the bar stool and screaming "Rape!" I'll bail him out tomorrow.

I got home at 4 A.M., tired, my head throbbing, my aura wilted. In the kitchen I cook some warm cocoa when I find, on the fridge, a note. This other-worldly missive is part love note, part reprimand. As audacious in familiarity as it is touching in juvenility. In simple block lettering it reads: "Next time, let us know when you'll be out late, so we don't have to stay up all night worrying that some other race is mating with you." These Pleiadians are acting more like Earth men every day!

"ABDUCTEE IN U.S.A."
New Punk Rock Song
(to the tune of The Sex Pistols' "Anarchy in the U.K.")

I am a devotee
of spirituality.

I read the tarot.
I've seen UFOs.
I want an alien to take me in tow!

'Cause I wanna be an abductee!

(no gravity for me!)

An abductee society
Is coming for you—wait and see.

We don't wanna defile or revile
We'd walk a million miles for the *X-Files!*

'Cause we—we wanna be abductees!

(on TV!)

Many ways to join the club
I use a psychotropic shrub.

I'm a pacifist and a humanist
I'm the alien's publicist!

'Cause I wanna be an abductee!

(It's the only way to be!)

Is you an Alien Gray?
And is you going away?

Can I be a stowaway?
Or is this the CIA?

Or just another doomsday?

(another chance to fly away!)

I wanna be an abductee!
And I wanna be an abductee!
And I wanna be an abductee!
(know what I mean?)
And I wanna be
an abductee!

Please take me!
Please take me!

COW MUTILATIONS
Intergalactic poaching, terror tactics or just a late night snack?

You've seen the *National Enquirer* headlines: UFOs LINKED TO WEIRD ANIMAL MUTILATIONS! You've seen the gruesome photographs. And, if you've ever visited my local Vietnamese restaurant, you've even tasted the results. We're talking unexplained cow mutilations!

You're a farmer who runs out into the field after hearing strange noises just in time to see a UFO flying off into the distance. And there, not more than twenty feet in front of you, lies the discarded carcasses of Bessie and Tessie, your two beloved heifers. They have been surgically dissected, their tongues, eyes, and sex organs removed with what your vet can only describe as the Rokitansky standard autopsy procedure (usually reserved for forensic cases). That eliminates the possibility of blaming your teenage son's Marilyn Manson records. In fact, the only other clue to the mystery is your farm's proximity to the local air force base. Wait, what's that sound? A low-flying black helicopter buzzes you. It starts to descend. In a moment you fear you will be the next living autopsy victim!

Scenarios like this one are as common as abductee reports and just as uniform. And although investigations as recent as 1994 concluded only with a recommendation to probe into satanic cults, there's definitely some high weirdness going on here that involves more than candles, incense, and bad medieval poetry. A New Mexican farmer saw one of his cows moving through the air, pulled by some unseen tractor beam. Some autopsies concluded that several other carcasses were airlifted, then dropped on the land in places where they would most likely be discovered. These include some of the United States' most secure military installations, like NORAD. Either these are some alien's idea of cow-tipping, or someone is rubbing the military's nose in the proverbial cow patty. The brilliant (but French) astrophysicist Jacques Vallee suggests that these incidents could be part of a domestic terror campaign waged by our own intelligence community. Many farmers believe that the government is conducting massive experiments, testing new drugs on their cows (and this at a time when there are so many lawyers running around loose?). One farmer's son experienced bizarre medical problems after coming in contact with a mutilated cow. Maybe this is a continuation of Gulf War Syndrome where, since the end of active combat for American troops, the government still needs its human guinea pigs as it did in World War II with nuclear bombs, in Vietnam with Agent Orange, and in the Gulf War with God knows what. Or maybe aliens are involved. And from the looks of it, they are either militant antivegetarians or off-planet medical school administrators looking for some cheap lab specimens.

FOO FIGHTERS

Today Antarctica, tomorrow the world, or Close Encounters of the Third Reich.

Toward the end of World War II British and American pilots reported being dogged on their flights by small balls of light. These luminescent orbs were often seen in groups of ten, darting around Allied airplanes like Kamikaze Tinker Bells. All this at a time when "UFO" could only have meant "Unidentified Führer Overhead"! Because these suspicious flying objects were believed to be secret German weapons they were called Foo Fighters, Feuerballs, or just plain Kraut Balls (or, in Hitler's case, Kraut Ball). Their origin and purpose still remain a mystery, so naturally there's more speculation surrounding Foo Fighters than the far too many spectral appearances of Elvis.

According to declassified CIA files, "Project Paperclip" imported over six hundred top Nazi scientists from Germany after the war, several of whom conducted "medical" experiments at Dachau (ones that make alien abduction seem like a waltz on the Reichstag). Many of their fun clinical procedures at the death camps were gasoline and mescaline injections, terminal ice-water baths, and high-altitude pressure chambers designed to crush the victim to death. So, naturally Uncle Sam saw their vast potential and recruited them in the service of the Cold War. These unreformed Nazis in lab coats not only assisted the CIA in dosing unsuspecting U.S. citizens with LSD but also transferred many advanced German weapons technologies for America's more mundane purpose of interballistic killing. Some of these airborne weapons, if one believes the speculations, were disc-shaped and capable of reaching speeds of 2,000 kilometers per hour at 12,400 meters in altitude. Pretty impressive for a country whose brain trust still wasn't smart enough to copyright Schindler's life story.

It seems likely that none of these German secret weapons survived the fall of the Third Reich and were supposedly destroyed during the Allied onslaught. Some right-wing theories claim that they did survive and are functioning well in secret Nazi camps in the South Pole. "Is that an incoming missile? No, it's an incoming Penguin—and he's wearing jackboots!" The Suppressed Technology Theory argues that these manmade UFOs got into the hands of the U.S. and Canadian governments and have been incorporated in the designs of many advanced weapons systems like the Stealth bomber and others known only to a few Pentagon officials and Republican finance officers. Like a phoenix rising from the ashes, Nazi UFOs may be seen in a sky near you funded by secret weapons budgets and presided over by You-Know-Who ("Hitler in 2000: Rested, Tan, and Ready!").

Signs of this coming Fourth Reich have already been seen as decals on many UFOs:

"Aryans on Board"

"Pleiades Uber Alles"

"I Brake for Pat Buchanan"

"Honk If You Love Bizarre and Inhuman Medical Experiments"

"How Am I Driving? Call 1-800 I LUV LAMPSHADES"

"Mercedes-Benz Crafters: World Domination in About an Hour"

THE MEN IN BLACK
(Secret Government Operatives, or Interstellar Seventh-Day Adventists?)

More controversy surrounds the ephemeral Men in Black than whether Harry Truman made a secret deal with the aliens or whether Ronald Reagan was an alien himself (and that after he served his purpose they took away his memory). Dressed like FBI men from the early '60s, these darkly clad figures act like automatons on Prozac—confiscating film, pieces of crashed UFOs, and sometimes witnesses. Some speculate that these men in black (or "MIBs") originate from the early days of the Atomic Energy Commission, whose mission it was to dispose of some of the nasty radioactive residues by dumping them into lakes, rivers, and streams (this was before the EPA and its insistence that the corporations do all the dumping themselves). On one particular June day in 1947, for example, six UFOs were sighted over Maury Island in Washington State. There was an explosion and flakes of silver and hunks of slag fell into the water. The MIBs arrived shortly thereafter and took the debris with them on a B-25—which promptly exploded minutes after takeoff. (Who says the government is inefficient?)

There are others who suggest that MIBs are aliens themselves, stomping out witnesses and their stories like a flamenco dancer on an anthill. Whatever is true, it appears that the Men in Black may have outlived their usefulness, which could be why there are fewer reports of them today. In a way, it's a pity. Some of the livelier sightings report pairs of MIBs driving vintage cars wearing their typical drab suites, but also topped with heavy makeup and full lipstick. Either they are slightly befuddled about our

The Official Alien Abductee's Handbook

sexual protocols, or they just never abducted a real drag queen with any sense of style or color. Or maybe they're subsidizing the rising expense of intergalactic travel by hawking surplus Avon products.

THE SPACE BROTHERS

Peace and harmony for all eternity—or just a one-night stand with some cosmic pimps?

The Space Brothers are kind, benevolent aliens, looking for an emissary to spread the gospel of their doting groovy intentions. Their envoys are chosen at random (from the looks of them) and are stricken with a timely and portent message to deliver to the sleepy people of Earth. The ambassador is then set off on the path to peace, love, and harmony, which is filled with widespread and constant public ridicule (but who said reaching bliss would be painless?). However, if you can gather enough true believers (and a hot-shot agent), the world tours will help take the edge off the incessant derision.

While the teachings of these cosmic masters are often sound and desirable (the prevention of nuclear war, the clean-up of the environment) some of their followers' beliefs are a few cliploads short of David Koresh. The Aetherius Society, for example, claims to control jumbo-size supplicant batteries that transmit powerful prayers to troubled spots in the world; the mostly disbanded Guardians believed they would be taken aboard alien space ships shortly before the coming apocalypse.

All religions have their kooky side, however, so we shouldn't be so quick to throw the fetus out with the semiotic fluid. Consider an established, reputable world religion such as Christianity. It holds to many elegant and decorous beliefs like the virgin birth and the transmutation of the blood and body of Christ from mass-produced table wine and stale cookie wafers, while our Space Brothers, on the other hand, wear cool jumpsuits and engage in group sex. Doesn't believing in them, upon comparison, seem less foolish (and more fun)? (It's a lot less foolish than believing that the government really doesn't know anything about UFOs.)

JOE SIMONTON'S INTERGALACTIC HOUSE OF PANCAKES

The man, the legend, the pancakes.

Nineteen sixty-one was a year when legends were made: Soviet cosmonaut Yuri Gagarin became the first man in space, V. S. Naipaul wrote *A House for Mr. Biswas*, and sixty-year-old farmer Joe Simonton seized the mantle of alien culinary achievement. It was late in the morning of April 18 when Joe saw a thirty-foot-long saucer hovering in his yard. Inside the craft were three beings who "resembled Italians"—not only for their dark hair and smarmy skin, but also in their love of cooking. One of the beings held up an empty jug, in the apparently universal sign of "Fill 'er up, Joe!" In a move that revealed his innate culinary skills and foreshadowed the start of his career in cookery, Joe took the jug into his house and promptly filled it with water. Upon his return he discovered the beings feverishly whipping up something on a grill inside their ship. He asked to try some of the food and was presented with three pancakes. Joe must have walked in during dessert, for the beings took off in the craft shortly after, leaving Joe with an example of extraterrestrial haute cuisine—and an empty stomach.

Joe had the pancakes analyzed by the U.S. Department of Health, Education and Welfare's food and drug laboratory, who found nothing otherworldly in them. The aliens must all be on a low sodium diet for there wasn't a trace of salt found—or tasted (as we know it). Quote Joe, who ate one of the pancakes, "It tasted like cardboard."

This appetizing episode of intergalactic cookery has inspired the following recipes:

COLD PASTA WITH IMPLANTS

Heat 3 cups water to boil in cold-fusion minireactor. Throw in noodles, with two tablespoons butter and NO SALT! Drain, cool, top with light peanut sauce, grated cheese, and long-distance, nano-powered tracking implants. Offer free with any delivery over ten thousand light-years.

CIA'S COVER-UP CASSEROLE

In total darkness open two cans of tomato sauce; remove and destroy the cans and the labels. Combine tomato sauce with water, onion, cheese, oregano, and sand from Roswell, New Mexico. Pour mixture into downed alien spacecraft (remember to remove the dead bodies first!). Heat with nuclear fission till only the spacecraft remains. Then photograph the results and hide all negatives and photos in a secret bunker in Alamogordo, New Mexico.

TESTICLES JAMBALAYA

Cut, slice, and dice four sets of human testicles, being careful to save the drained fluid in a separate bowl. Cook skins in olive oil in deep skillet with green peppers and garlic until crisp. Lace skins together into sexual talismans. With basting syringe suck up the semen and fertilize sterile female aliens while dancing in a frenzied circle as Ravel's "Bolero" plays.

DIVINE INVASIONS

The celestial chorus from above brings enlightenment—in chains.

Before there were abductees there were contactees. No, these were not humans infected by alien venereal disease (that's another chapter), but humans whose claimed interaction with aliens led them to change their lives, promote world peace, and, if they were lucky, enabled them to start a cult with generous followers.

Like most true believers, contactees see their philosophy in every prophecy. For them ET intervention is evidenced everywhere from Jesus (his ascension from the dead is proof that tractor beams from spacecraft really do work) to Mother Theresa (do we really have to note her wrinkled resemblance to the Grays?). And contactees, like Mother Theresa, also collect money for good deeds.

The beginnings of various contactee cults are rooted, not surprisingly, in the occult:

— The I AM movement was founded in the early 1930s by Guy and Edna Ballard who claimed to channel "Venusians" as diverse as "The Lord of the Flame" to Jesus himself. Many of their followers were recruited from the Silver Shirts, a group formed by William Dudley Pelley, famous American fascist. This set the tone for future cults: a lot of mysticism, a little loopiness, and a whole lotta subservience.

— George Adamski wrote the seminal *Flying Saucers Have Landed* in 1953, claiming he had years of alien contacts. He also claimed he was a professor associated with Mount Palomar, but later admitted to only slinging grilled burgers in a nearby tourist café on the slopes. He allegedly confessed to Ray Stanford, UFO researcher and former follower, that he formed the Sacred Order of Tibet during Prohibition as a front for bootlegging wine. "If it hadn't been for that son-of-a-bitch man Roosevelt," he was quoted as saying, "I wouldn't have to get into all this saucer crap."

— Daniel Fry was a missile engineer at the White Sands Proving Ground when he witnessed the landing of a huge flying saucer. He was about to touch the hull when a voice from inside warned him: "Better not touch the hull, pal, it's still hot!" That voice belonged to A-Lan the alien (Alan for short) who told him to warn the people of Earth against nuclear wars. Again traces of the American fascist movement can be seen to have influenced this and the I AM movement, where Venusians occupy the highest rank in the "Great White Brotherhood," with Aryans the highest native race on Earth. This goes a long way in explaining contactees' fascination with jackboots, black shirts, paranoia, and an exclusive membership policy beloved by rich, white Republican golfers.

The philosophical descendants of the contactees are those alien abductees who have been instructed by aliens to turn away from the material, seek the spiritual, and work for a world government where your DNA is your only passport. This new nation has a new slogan: "Love and revere life, or become extinct!"

These optimistic abductees believe that all those stories of forced abductions by aggressive and menacing aliens are part of a deliberate government disinformation campaign to spread fear and mistrust in the aliens and to justify a Star Wars weapons buildup against the "Gray Menace." "My fellow Americans, we have met the enemy and he is *ugly!*"

True aliens, these believers say, are loving, caring creatures who themselves believe in a Supreme Being. But for cynics, nonbelievers, and self-employed taxpayers who hear the phrase, "God works in mysterious ways," the response is, "So did the Marquis de Sade and Charles Manson!"

PREPARING FOR THE INEVITABLE
Make no mistake—*you* are the designated donor!

Elizabeth Kubler-Ross said it best when she outlined the stages one faces when one faces death. The same applies to you, my dear abductee, when you face the inevitable. Anger, fear, denial, bargaining, and acceptance—you must pass through all these stages before joining a club so exclusive some people are members for years without even knowing it.

Anger: Spend countless nights held against your will being subjected to painful medical procedures, returned naked and scarred like ditched meat, and you too might feel a little miffed. Most people need to feel wanted, but this makes solitary confinement look like Club Med.

Fear: Sure, your abductors are all-powerful and play it from the dominant end of the probe, but you have your fear to comfort you. If you weren't afraid you would have to be completely unaware of your recurring nightmares, numerous scoop marks, and other signs of privilege. Remember that your fear assures you of your own living, breathing existence, which is subject to recall at any time by its legal proprietor. Let the fear flow through you and before you know it you'll arrive at the next stage.

Denial: It's all too painful to be real, but it's all too real to be faced—so just avoid it all. As those memories of abduction bubble up to the surface threatening to tear the very fabric of your underlying reality—just tell your unconscious mind what Harry Truman told his military officers when presented with evidence of a UFO crash: "Suppress it!" Follow the advice of our protective government officials: deny, deny, deny! And when you have exhausted your capacity to deny, move ahead to your next stage on the evolutionary chessboard:

Bargaining: "Just let me get through the weekend—or at least through the Interstate—without being abducted and I swear I'll send in my contribution to the Sierra Club." Or, "If you must scoop my skin, try to do it within my tan lines." Or, "Take my lover, my mother, my children—just leave *me* alone!!" None of these bargaining ploys, however, will work. And, deep down, you know it. Which is why you must come finally to:

Acceptance: After all, you are special. Why else would they have chosen you? Not for your insight into human nature, nor for your political connections, and certainly not for your good looks. No one can say why exactly you were chosen, so just accept the fact that you are special, and that your life does have a purpose. Then you can finally be at peace with the knowledge that of all the millions of individual life forms in the universe, you were picked to be the designated donor for a troop of aliens caught DWI (Driving While Interbreeding).

THE PSYCHOLOGICAL PROFILE OF AN ET ABDUCTOR

Know thyself, know thy abductor, know the nearest exit.

Cosmic understanding is a strong and powerful force in the universe. For an abductee it's almost strong enough to alleviate the pain, fear, humiliation, and intermittent radio signals blaring those annoying Honda commercials in your head. The truly evolved abductee, however, will acknowledge feelings of hurt without dwelling on them. You too can gain a greater acceptance by studying this psychological profile of your abductors (prepared by a team of professional therapists, Ufologists, and Louis my chiropractor).

A typical ET abductor has no real mother or father, just intergalactic sperm zipping through space without a condom. Because of this lack of familial bonds, they are deprived. They compensate for this giant gaping hole in the pit of their being by suppressing all feeling and emotion. This makes them more volatile than Jeffrey Dahmer on a protein-free diet.

With an average life span of more than three thousand years, the alien abductor has a wealth of experience of other planets and species. The problem is, most of those were spent looking for love in all the wrong places. Because of this peripatetic wanderlust, the ET whiles the time away in lonely frustration running out of available species to slaughter and planets to destroy. Their telepathic communication skills only heighten their dysfunctional relationship with you: The uncontrolled fear they read inside your mind they interpret as an endearing coyness. ETs may be intellectually advanced, but they are more emotionally stunted than an anorexic fashion model at an all-day shoot for Ben & Jerry's.

In case you haven't guessed it, the alien abductor's biggest problem is fear of intimacy, which is why they hide behind skin-scooping needles and sterilized probes. This fear can quickly turn pathological, manifesting itself with a wanton disregard of personal property—like your life. But just because they show no guilt, it doesn't mean they don't deserve to live out the rest of their miserable and pathetic lives in the middle of a black hole with twelve thousand Freudian analysts.

HOW TO ABDUCT YOUR VERY OWN ALIEN
For fun, profit, or just plain revenge.

For those with an adventurous bent (or for those just excessively bent) nothing quite matches the thrill of alien stalking: the long watchful hours spent waiting in an abandoned city dump; the stillness of the predawn, disturbed only by the wild thumping in your primitive mammalian heart; the adrenaline rush at the first sighting—your potential captors are now your prey! You have set your decoy: a mannequin dressed in flannel coveralls adorned with two six-packs and an orange cap with I AM THE NRA stitched on the front. The aliens approach the decoy and attempt to paralyze it with their flash-ray guns. Here's where you spring into action, releasing the trap provided in your Official Alien Abductor's Toolkit. The trap raises a seven-foot full-length mirror that reflects back the aliens' ray-guns, paralyzing *them* instead. Later, while driving your pickup with an alien or two strapped to the front grill, you can be heard shouting: "I love the smell of ectoplasm in the morning!" The alien is now yours, to do with what you will. A memorable day indeed, whether you're a bounty hunter, game preservationist, or just an aficionado of kinky sex.

ALIEN INFILTRATORS IN OUR CULTURE
How to mass market a successful alien inva—uh, campaign.

"Xenob and Gentle-entities, we have here the results from our focus group. While the awareness of your species has greatly increased—thanks in part to the successful abduction of all talk-show hosts—your image is not quite as consumer-friendly as it could be. In fact, it's just plain threatening. Now, before we all fly off the saucer, let me interject a personal anecdote that may shed some light on the challenge: I was at the mall shopping with my darling daughter yesterday, when she asked: 'Daddy, can I have Rusty Root Canal?' I turned and saw a tooth-shaped clown doll hanging in the window, beckoning my kid to snap him and cuddle him while she gets drilled senseless at her next dental visit. Think of it! Hundreds of thousands of American kids doing their part for the toy and the medical markets! Now the same can be done for you folks, if we create the right image. Let Sheree here give you a visual demonstration of what I'm talking about. Sheree?"

"Thanks, Bob. Okay, guys, take a look at the first panel. It shows two little kids lost in the woods. In the next panel a friendly beacon of light shines down on them and leads them out to safety. Next we see an old woman whose husband is sick in bed. Again the light, and—whammo! he's not only cured, he grabs his wife and starts making out. The final frames show a sad couple looking at an empty bassinet. The loving white light glows in from the window, and when it fades a beautiful baby-child lays smiling before them. The voiceover speaks: 'The divine visit—heavy times call for light measures.' We end with the large smiling face of—well, you know, *you guys!*"

"Terrific, isn't it? Continue, Sheree."

"Okay, Bob, guys. Here we see a happy couple comfortably sleeping in the bedroom. Our loving, friendly light starts shining outside. But in this case, no one notices—except the family dog, who trots out to meet the saucer on the front lawn. A delicate three-fingered gray hand extends nonthreateningly out to the dog. Next panel shows the dog leading the visitors into the bedroom. Now we just see the couple's feet floating off the ground and out the window. The camera pans over to the nightstand and rests on the book called *Family Planning*. The loving gray hand pats the happy dog on its head as the voiceover reads: 'Be a friendly neighbor, let them borrow a cup.'

"Now, c'mon, guys, I think Sheree's done an excellent job here. And, frankly, short of midnight access to the water supply, you won't get a better chance than this! Now wait, back off, you guys, *back off* . . . !!!"

THE NEW AGE COMIC

A late-night transmission received from the Borscht Asteroid Belt

Thank you, thank you . . . . I'm not really the "New Age" comic, I just channel him while he's on tour. Actually, he was abducted by aliens, and couldn't get out of their management contract.

Anybody here from out of town? You, sir? Chicago? It's a great place to visit, but I wouldn't want to be abducted there.

Q: How many abductees does it take to screw in a lightbulb?
A: Three: two to screw it in, and one to breed with the aliens while the other two are distracted.

Q: How many abductees does it take to screw in a lightbulb?
A: It may have been shaped like a lightbulb, but it's really a spaceship.

Q: How many abductees does it take to screw in a lightbulb?
A: Just one. But it takes years of regressive hypnosis to remember screwing it in.

These are the jokes, folks. I know you're out there, 'cause I can see your auras.

Q: What do you get when you cross an alien with the Godfather?
A: An offer you can't refuse—again and again.

Q: What do you get when you cross an alien with a demon from hell?
A: Another alien.

You know what I hate about alien abductions? Not the physical fear, not the painful and bizarre medical experiments, not the lingering scars and lasting shame . . . no, I hate it that they never call you again in the morning. This girl I know, for example, she's been abducted four, maybe five times. Then [snaps fingers] like that they stopped. They even told her, "We have finished with you now, thank you, you must go." The kind of thing I used to say before I became enlightened. [fake cough] Anyway, this chick actually misses them. Kind of like the Stockholm syndrome where you identify with your captors—which is why she now wears clown-white makeup and snacks on insects. Anyway, she misses them and wants to see them again, so I told her, "Place an ad in the personals. Something like: 'Fertile Earth woman in search of one who is small, powerful, and dominant, and who likes to love 'em and leave 'em.'" Come to think of it, screw the ad—any bar in Queens will do!

Hey, buddy, you don't like what you see up here? Follow my bliss, pal. Abduct him if he can't take a joke!

THE STOCKHOLM SYNDROME
Make 'em have your babies, and they'll name 'em after you.

Isolation, fear, and dependency are the main fun tools of the aliens' indoctrination methods. Their scheme must surely rank, along with voluntary tax payments and depilatory commercials, as one of the greatest brainwashing fetes in modern history. It is quite similar to the Stockholm syndrome, not because of the aliens' resemblance to the Nordic race (though did you ever wonder about Renny Harlin?), but because of their success in converting many abductees (prisoners) into their belief system (political ideology) by way of controlling the basic survival needs of their captives—in other words, not just sending your brain to the cleaners, but dressing it in the swaddling clothes of a true believer (this goes a long way in explaining the vacant neophyte look in many New Agers).

For a successful indoctrination, all four human brain circuits must be sequentially washed. Like layers of ground-in dirt these circuits are not necessarily hard to wash, they just need repeated efforts and a sense of righteousness that would give Martha Stewart split ends.

These circuits are:
• The Biosurvival circuit: The infant level where basic survival needs of food, shelter, and comfort are fixated onto a mother figure. By isolating and restraining the abductee the aliens reduce the victim to a state of infantilized dependency not seen since the tobacco industry was threatened with subsidy cuts.

• The Ego circuit: The emotional toddler level where basic motor functions are tested and, in indoctrination schemes, subjugated. Despite the aliens' own shrimpiness, the abductee is made to feel smaller than worker dwarfs by means of terror tactics: intrusive medical procedures, involuntary mindscan, and the liberal use of entire muscular paralysis. The abductee thus feels more helpless than a voter on election day.

• The Mind circuit: The rational grade-school level where language and communication are learned. In the case of alien abductions, the abductee must learn an entirely new method of communication: The aliens telepathically send commands, and the abductee obeys.

• The Sociosexual circuit: The adult level concerned with personality and domestic behavior. For alien abductees (who have now lost their sense of security, independence, and previously cherished views of the universe) this can only mean one thing: *Alien Breeding!!!*

In this way the aliens are able to indoctrinate abductees with the same panache and flair the Symbionese Liberation Army used in brainwashing Patty Hearst, Charles Manson employed in recruiting his extended family members, and Disney uses to entice us into paying for that silly ride with the insidious song: "It's a Small World After All."

The message the aliens want to implant in us is the usual one: "Clean up your act." We apparently have been leading a life so devoid in spiritual awareness and so reckless in consideration of other living creatures (like our own planet) that their intervention (and better advertising through abductees) has been necessary. Once indoctrinated, abductees then spread the alien message of love, harmony, and expanded consciousness with the zealousness of true believers and the obedience of circus animals.

GENITALIA ENVY

Is that a phaser in your pocket or are you just happy to abduct me?

The aliens' abduction and breeding practices may stem from their own lack of genitalia—a psycho-physiological ailment that keeps them wrapped tighter than a classified government document. From the hundreds of investigated abduction cases not a single one reported any sightings of alien genitalia. Of course, staring at an ET's crotch may not be your first instinct when they have you strapped to an operating table, but you don't easily forget a captor who has the eyes of a grasshopper and the lap of a Barbie doll. It seems, therefore, highly probable that genitalia envy is the root cause of the aliens' antisocial behavior. Flying the intergalactic highways and byways, our ET neighbors may be more than envious when they witness our daily and nightly matings in the bedroom, office, car, and on *Baywatch*. Not only do they want to get in on the action, but (like all real moralists who feel left out) they want to teach us all a lesson. How else can you explain their quaint method of genetic coupling that rivals Leather Night at the Stone Anvil?

Despite their exacting and insensitive methods of interspecies breeding, the ETs may, deep down, have our best interests at heart. In this era of deadly sexually transmitted diseases, true safe sex may actually be exo-sex: designer sex performed with precision, purpose, and power tools.

ANGELS VS. ALIENS
All's fair in love, war, and publicity.

The New Age territory is growing and so are the stakes. Angels, aliens, and agents now slug it out in the publicity ring for a media prize bigger than a UFO crash landing at the Super Bowl. We're not just talking the hearts and minds of the population, but their very belief systems and, most important, their buying habits.

The contest pits the seraphically virtuous and beatifically sexy angels against the enigmatically nasty and incorrigibly randy aliens (at least that's how my publicity agent sees it). Angels and aliens now vie for the highest sales in T-shirts, books, bumper stickers, and 900 numbers. In this battle for media saturation, are the players evenly matched? And what exactly are they pitching, besides the essence of their own fatuous fabulousness?

For their part the angels are sent by the divine creator to guide and assist humankind in our evolutionary progress. As for the aliens, their intentions remain as shrouded as a military hanger in Nevada. By their actions, though, they have shown their fondness for midnight abductions, mind control, forced impregnations, and cute body scars. Not exactly the behavior guaranteed to make you as popular as Mother Theresa. If they were hawking perfume, the angels' scent would be a sweet combination of pink cotton candy with a lemon spritz—named "Rapture." The aliens' fragrance would be a bit of vintage musk with an injection of ectoplasmic sagebrush—named "Capture." At last count the aliens have recruited some of the most famous and powerful believers on planet Earth, including Jimmy Carter, Ross Perot, and even Minister Farrakhan, who had a vision of being taken aboard a UFO where he met Elijah Muhammad, Moses, Jesus, and other off-planet celebrities.

Perhaps not so curiously, many of these folk also believe in angels. Some state that aliens are actually angels in space clothing (which may allow them to be so aggressive). Consider the similarities: the appearance of bright white lights, the apparent exemption from the known laws of physics, the smug sense of superiority over mere mortals and their pets, and of course the overwrought concern for human fecundity. Just read this passage from the Bible: "And it came to pass, when men began to multiply on earth, and daughters were born unto them, that the Sons of God saw the daughters of men that they were fair; and they took them wives of all they chose" (Genesis 6: 1-3). (Why do those Sons of God always act like sailors on leave?) In a later passage they are referred to as "giants"— an inexact translation from the Hebrew word *Nephilum*—literally meaning fallen-down ones. And, unless you still consider those Sons of God to be AWOL lifers, "those who have fallen from above" could only point to you-know-who ("took them wives" indeed!).

So, are we witnessing a divine makeover by God on his cosmetically clichéd minions? Or could the alien phenomenon be simply a multimedia spinoff of that old chestnut—the battle between the forces of good and evil? As the angels/aliens war rages, the cost is more than just your soul—it's your pocketbook!

COMPARE THE EXPRESSIONS

Angels	Aliens
Angel face.	Aliens in your face.
Your Guardian Angel.	You're guarding against Aliens.
Where Angels fear to tread.	Where Aliens tread on you fearlessly.
A thousand Angels dancing on the head of a pin.	Aliens pinning you down a thousand times so you can't move your head, let alone dance.
Angel in my pocket.	Aliens pocketing you.
Angel cake.	Alien whipped soufflé (guess what it's whipped with and who does the whipping).

CHARIOTS OF THE CREEPS

Genetic experiment of the gods, or ancient folk tales in New Age clothing?

"The chariots of God are twenty thousand, even thousands of angels: the Lord is among them . . . " (Psalms 68:17) . . . and apparently he's a union buster!

According to linguist Zecharia Sitchin, when godlike visitors came to Earth over 450,000 years ago to exploit its natural resources (particularly gold) they needed extra help hauling their booty. So these gods created the working class and lo they saw that it was good, underpaid, underfed, and too scared of those beings who created them to unionize. Created them? Yeah, according to Sitchin's interpretation of ancient Summarian texts, these alien gods mixed their DNA with early proto-human species (monkeys, to you) to create Homo Sapiens (also called Domesticated Primates and Precursors to Pro Wrestling Fans). In this interpretation, Noah was actually Atra-hasis who received instruction to obtain, not animals two by two, but actual genetic material of the animals and place it aboard the Ark (this not only conserved space, but allowed Noah to receive large funding from the National Science Foundation to study the effects of seasickness on DNA molecules).

Author Erich von Daniken is credited with starting this trend in tracing the human family tree to outer space in his 1971 book *Chariots of the Gods?* (the question mark considered by many to be most appropriately placed). The aliens were responsible for our evolution, Daniken claims. How else can you explain the fifty-foot, fifty-ton Easter Island statues erected on an island without even trees to roll them on or Kevin Costner to sign the paychecks?

Appearances by godlike creatures dot the Bible like UFO blips across an astronaut's windshield. Combining "celestial chariots," angels, and other mystical apparitions along with paternalistic dogma, the good book often reads like L. Ron Hubbard on steroids. Four hundred years ago religious theologians sweated about the incubi and succubi—demons who seduce men and women, often forcing them to have their babies, and, even worse, eat their pancakes (*De Delictis et Poenis* by Fr. Ludovicus Maria Sinistrari de Ameno . . . look it up yourself!).

The Celtic legends speak of elves, fairies, pixies, wee folk, and goblins who abduct pregnant women and young mothers, steal their babies, and substitute a changeling for the real child. The chronically French scientist Jacques Vallee painstakingly traced the parallels between these legends, religious apparitions, and current UFO encounters with some intriguing results. Take fairy rings, for example (I don't mean jewelry given during San Franciscan civil ceremonies by same sex-partners): they look an awful lot like crop circles and burnt grass after a UFO landing. These visitors may have progressed from fairy wands to zap guns, but they haven't lost their taste for abductions. The Alien Golden Rule seems to be: Do unto others—over and over again.

Where do they come from? Are the wee folk masters of an ancient civilization that has coexisted with us for decades, or are they just an overflow from last week's St. Patty's Day parade? Do strange visitors live in a universe parallel to ours, and do they come to visit us for company, communication, and interspecies dating? We may never know if we carry in our genes the seed of the gods, the breath of the angels, or the love note from some gnome.

THE OFFICIAL ALIEN ABDUCTEE HOTLINE

Call 1-900-PROBE-ME

"Hello, and thank you for calling 1-900-Probe-Me. The cost of this call is only $5.99/per minute. If you are under eighteen, or have never been abducted, please hang up now. 1-900-Probe-Me is the premiere service for interstellar connections, companionship, and survivor support. Press One now if you want to listen to true-life abduction stories from around the world and beyond. Press Two now if you want to leave a message for our alien visitors (maximum limit of twenty-three profane words). Press Three now to order our special edition of *Scoop Dreams Magazine*, the finest in full-color, full-frontal documentation. Press Four now if you want to talk live one on one with Ted Blotter—internationally renown psychic and cosmetics adviser. Press Five now if you want to hear dirty confessions of exotically close alien encounters of the extremely intimate kind. Press Six now to schedule a transpersonal session with a metaphysical massage therapist. Press Seven now to seek shelter in one of our finely appointed secret underground bunkers. Press Eight if you are a member of the intelligence community and want to obtain a mailing list of our bunker residents. Press Nine if you want to receive a shipment of your very own hybrid baby farm—just add carbonated water and watch 'em grow like sea monkeys in a fecal swamp."

LAST EXIT TO ROSWELL

The story of an alien, a saucer, and some friendly military folk with a lot of explaining to do.

You're thousands of light-years from home, alone and experiencing vehicle failure. You crash on a planet that has just discovered nuclear energy and has just as quickly unleashed two atomic bombs . . . if you ever get your hands on that travel agent you'd show them what you can do with a probe! That could have been the experience of the unknown alien whose saucer crashed near Roswell, New Mexico, in 1947. Or it could all be just another fable in the modern mythology of UFOria. If it wasn't for that puzzling evidence . . .

William "Mac" Brazel and his seven-year-old neighbor Dee Proctor discover the remains of a crashed flying saucer on a ranch on July 3, 1947. These remains could neither be blow-torched nor flattened by any method tried. Of course, the army confiscated all remaining pieces and put out an official statement saying what crashed was a "weather balloon." The only thing that contradicted this was its previous statement saying it had found the remains of a crashed flying saucer.

Not that anyone really took much notice of the army's official denials. No one, except for Mac Brazel and family. Mac spent the next week in constant military escort, after which time he too learned how to officially deny. (He did get a large freezer out of the deal, however.)

Glenn Dennis got nothing but the boot. Dennis worked for a mortuary. Around July 9, 1947, he received several phone calls from an administrator in Roswell Army Air Field who asked him about hermetically sealed caskets ("What's the smallest one they could get?"). He was also asked about chemical solutions. Either the army was planning to ship recovered alien bodies in these caskets or they were blowing their mid-year budget on some bizarre party favors.

One day while Dennis was trying to nail some foxy nurse at Roswell Army Hospital he got more rejection than he bargained for. On his way to the Coke machine he passed the wreckage of the spaceship. It was guarded by two MPs who performed a move on Dennis quicker than the move he planned for the nurse. The MPs even followed him back to the funeral home, and, unlike what Dennis would have done for the nurse, called him just a few hours later saying, "You open your mouth and you'll be so far back in the jug they'll have to shoot pinto beans into you with a bean shooter." (Obviously an illusive reference to alien anal probes.) The next day the nurse told Dennis the hospital had three dead alien bodies in storage and ready to be shipped. If they were revived and where they were shipped is anybody's guess, but did you ever notice the otherworldly glaze in the eyes of Disneyland employees?

Major Jesse Marcel took a few souvenirs from the wreckage. After all, these are some of the perks of a military job—and arriving early on the scene. Jesse summoned his wife and son at two o'clock in the morning to view the remnants he spread out on their living room floor. This unusual and early Christmas ritual included attempts to bend, burn, and pummel the pieces—all to no apparent damage. Ever the obedient soldier, Jesse returned all the pieces to the army, leaving his son to wonder what to expect when the real Christmas finally comes to the Marcel home.

Since those carefree days thousands of outraged, curious, or merely bored U.S. citizens have demanded an official answer to the Roswell mystery. In July of 1995, the Government Accounting Office filed a report on the crash and concluded that, over forty years ago, most official Air Force communication documents concerning the crash "were destroyed without proper authority." This is the kind of stuff that separates the truly paranoid from the merely skeptical. The Air Force would admit only that the crashed vehicle was a then-classified device "to detect evidence of possible Soviet nuclear testing." Makes you wonder what other toys the government is currently hiding ("Lockheed's new Roswell Saucer Escort—it takes you where you want to go— and leaves you there in little pieces.") News like this will stop you from buying that cheap house downwind from a U.S. military installation—you know, the one performing alien autopsies.

AN ALIEN AT MY (AUTOPSY) TABLE
Scalpel, suture, lights, camera, action!

Like a scrappy vampire with #500 sunblock, the Roswell legend is hard to kill. Through sci-fi books and movies and clunky hoaxes, those little gray corpses in Hanger 18 will always have someone championing for their release—or just acknowledgment.

Consider the curious Majestic 12 report. The MJ-12 report is an alleged highly classified U.S. document that mentions the recovery of dead aliens at Roswell. The document was stamped with a large "eyes only" headline followed by several paragraphs that looked like they were typed on a scavenged Smith-Corona from Ted Kaczynski's cabin. After much analysis, however, MJ-12 is now widely viewed to be as undoctored as a Beverly Hills breast.

Hoaxes have a long tradition in the UFO field. And hoaxing hard-core believers is as difficult as tripping a blind man. So, when a film showing a purported autopsy performed on a Roswell alien appeared on the scene in 1995, many once-burned UFOlogists looked closely and cried "Foul!" (or is it "Flying unknown winged entity"?)

When this now-infamous footage was introduced on the Fox Network in the United States there followed a feeding frenzy not seen since Clinton visited a Kentucky Fried Chicken factory. After viewing the film one pathologist said that "the prosecutor used scissors like a tailor, not like a pathologist or surgeon." But how does he know the surgeon wasn't a tailor? Maybe there wasn't enough time to find a real surgeon. This experience probably influenced the tailor and several fashion trends from then on. How else can you explain Jean-Paul Gaultier?

Other criticisms cited the lack of connecting tissue found inside the "alien." In fact, the guts of the creature looked like they came from a Santería Bodega.* Another comment from a prominent Hollywood special-effects creator noted that the alien figure was a dummy cast in an upright position. (This would explain why it looks as lifelike as a Muppet stuffed with canceled checks from the Pentagon's lunch tab.) The result, perhaps, of either too much armature in the dummy, or too much liquid coolant in the extra-terresty.

*Santería is a religion imported from the Yoruba of West Africa when they were brought to Cuba as slaves. They preserved their religious heritage by disguising their gods as Catholic saints (a practice many merchandisers here do during Christmas). Santería is a blend of primitive magic and Catholicism now practiced by 5 million Hispanic Americans. Some of the rituals include animal sacrifices. A bodega is a small store found on the corners of many Hispanic communities. There one can purchase cigarettes, sodas, candy, crack cocaine, and small live animals for religious get-togethers.

Regardless of your opinion on the authenticity of the alien autopsy film, no one can deny the usefulness of the following list:

TEN USES FOR A DEAD ALIEN

Buy 'em, collect 'em, trade 'em, be hunted down by unmarked government helicopters for 'em!

1) As a prop for a Phony Alien Autopsy Film
   (or a lost *X-Files* episode).
2) When you put a wig on it, it looks like Larry King—and
   hosts an even better talk show!
3) As featured in the new Disneyland theme ride: "Beauty
   and the Beast with a Ten-inch Probe"!
4) As a fashion model for the cover of the *Weekly World News*.
5) As a medical aid for Lamaze classes.
6) As the pro-life poster child.
7) As the surprise third-party presidential candidate.
8) As a weathervane that always points up.
9) As a mascot for the North American Man-Boy
   Love Association.
10) As a NASA hood ornament.

A DREAMLAND OF DOLLARS

At Area 51 they know how to keep warm on a cold night—throw another alien on the toxic waste fire!

If you're now worried about the presence of aliens in your life, just wait till you hear what the U.S. government does with your tax dollars in the name of national security. At a secret Air Force facility in Nevada, a recent lawsuit alleges, open pits the size of football fields are filled regularly with toxic waste, doused with jet fuel, then set ablaze—while workers stand downwind from this potent, and illegal, cocktail. This ethically challenged barbecue takes place in Area 51 (also known as Groom Lake, Dreamland, Paradise Ranch, and The Place Where Uniformed Men Come to Take You Away if You Wander Too Close).

Funded to the tune of $22 billion plus as part of the federal government's "black budget" (and I don't mean military minstrel shows), Groom Lake has produced such super-secret weapons as the U-2 spy plane and the F-117A "stealth" fighter-bomber. But it's not just the parade of overpriced jock toys that brings UFO watchers there nightly. It is rumored that, deep in the bowels of this complex of hangars and radar dishes, beyond the world's longest runway, nestled behind the swimming pool, bowling alley, bars, and X-rated movie lounges frequented by military brass and fighter jockeys, is the deepest secret our government has ever lied about. No, not the actual cost of a Pentagon hammer, but actual alien spacecraft. Here top military scientists purportedly disassemble recovered flying saucers to unearth the secrets of UFO technology (including, one hopes, the device that allows aliens to fly directly over U.S. military installations at speeds exceeding 55 mph without once being pulled over).

But all is not well in Dreamland. And the government, once again, is blamed for using the cover of Ufology to disguise its nefarious, illegal, and downright smelly shenanigans. The lawsuit names the Defense Department, the Air Force, and the National Security Agency, all which at first denied the very existence of Area 51. Then attorney Jonathan Turley threatened to submit declassified Soviet satellite photos to prove its existence. Turley, who works for the Washington-based Environmental Crimes Project, blames the Environmental Protection Agency for not monitoring waste disposal at the facility. The EPA, for its part, first said it could not enforce the law at an installation that does not exist. It now grudgingly admits having only recently "inventoried" the Groom Lake facility. ("Let's see, that's 2,034 empty fifty-five-gallon drums, 113 spent rocket fuel cannisters, and 59,023 boxes of bar matches.")

In response to mounting public awareness and this recent lawsuit, the government finally capitulated and did what it had to do— seize four thousand acres of public land surrounding Area 51—in the name of national security, of course. And if this modern Machiavellian move manages to keep us from looking in, we can only imagine the frightful, untold secrets that remain hidden. Consider recent American history: the Atomic Energy Commission experimenting on unsuspecting Americans in the '40s, the CIA conducting LSD experiments on unsuspecting Americans in the '60s, and who knows what type of Mengele-inspired experiments the military subjected unsuspecting American soldiers to during Desert Storm. Wonder why they call it national security? Because it is easy to nationally secure a disinformed and diseased population—and even easier to collect their taxes.

ALIEN ABDUCTEE GLOSSARY

Alien—One who abducts you for unknown purposes, without ransom or media attention.

Abductions—Repeated periods of captivity by aliens usually accompanied by intense medical experimentation, sexual subjugation, and electronic implantation. Not recommended.

Abductee—One who gets abducted and whose life will never be the same again. Valid until death.

Anarchist—See "Alien."

Bedroom—1) at home: a place where you await abductions; 2) on a spacecraft: the operating facility; 3) after abductions: usually an abandoned field.

Blue Book, Project—The U.S. Air Force's fairy tales.

Cattle mutilation—Fast food.

Central Intelligence Agency—The only government organization entrusted with the true secret of the alien invDELETED

Children—Bargaining chips.

Close Encounters of the Third Kind—The New Age version of *Triumph of the Will*.

Dreams—Fantastic images of space creatures and life-threatening adventures that occur during a normal sleep (that's what you think!).

ETs—Endlessly Testing Sadists.

Friends—People you turn to for solace, sympathy, and support —until you tell them the truth.

Government—A loose organization of conspirators, defended by military power, protected by lying bureaucrats, and dedicated to the continuation of a terrorist state. (Also applies to nonalien forms of government.)

Hell—A place of perpetual torment unencumbered by the prospect of abductions. Recommended.

Insomnia—1) The normal state of waiting for abductions. 2) A perfect time to reflect on your blessings. 3) An extremely short time.

Jealousy—What other people feel toward you when they discover you are an abductee. (Keep repeating this to yourself!)

Karma—The sum and consequences of a person's actions usually repaid during another phase of a person's existence. Example: For every four abductions, an abductee gets to appear once on a talk show.

Loser—See "Abductee."

Mercy—What you don't get from your abductor.

New Age—The burgeoning new utopian era when mysteries will be revealed and your most intimate experiences will be syndicated on all 500 channels.

Official Investigation—Sanctioned cover-up designed to confuse an already unstable society while distracting the public from the government's own nefarious activities.

Psychologist—Someone who will listen to your troubles and help you integrate and accept your abductions so that you can undergo them with grace and frequency. Psychologists actually think they are doing you good.

Quota—The number of abductees assigned by the aliens to be abducted before they call it quits. Whatever this unknown number is, you're far from being off the list.

Regressive hypnosis—A prolonged and expensive therapy used to either extract or implant hidden memories of exotic abuse. Patients receive emotional support through the special privilege of being chosen by aliens—and written about in the therapist's next published book.

Relief— s - u - i - c - i - d - e . . .

Scoop marks—Hickeys given to abductees by their alien abductors. Shows they care, and, because they medically test you before they breed with you, that they are careful, too.

Spouse—Someone you apologize to for your long absences.

Support group—A gathering of other abductees where misery is shared, body scars compared, and a government infiltrator is the laird.

Time travel—Purported method of transportation utilized by the aliens in the quest for human specimens, and the premise of many bad science-fiction movies.

UFOs—Civilian name given to limousine service run by unlicensed offshore medical practitioners.

Vacation—That all-too-brief time between abductions.

War of the Worlds—The coming intergalactic gladiator games.

X-Files—A popular documentary TV show.

Zoo —Where missing abductees go.

ABOUT THE AUTHOR

Joe Tripician started writing alien stories at age six on the walls of his parents' house in Margate, New Jersey. Seeing his natural talent, his mom and dad encouraged him to go into sports. He rebelled at age thirteen, appropriated his dad's movie camera, and shot sci-fi epics in the backyard. By high school he was performing on the stage. By college he discovered where the stage lights were and continued to make twisted films through his years at American University and Columbia University. After torturing Muppets for two years as Jim Henson's production assistant, Joe started his own New York–based film and TV production company, Co-Directions, Inc., and made several occult-inspired documentaries for PBS with partner Merrill Aldighieri. After winning his first EMMY (for the documentary *Metaphoria*) Joe began writing alien stories again. This time he uses paper, pencil, and, occasionally, a computer.

FRIGHTENED? WORRIED? ANGRY? OR JUST HUNGRY FOR MORE?

Visit the Official Alien Abductee's Website: The Ultimate Self-Help URL for the New Millennium for advice, truths, hidden conspiracies, and a blast of alien rock music: "Melodies for Abductees."

Meet and interact with a star therapist, a professional abductee, a loud-mouthed skeptic, a raving cult leader, and your master, Xenob the High Pleiadian at *www.uexpress.com/alien-abductee/*.